raise your line

SUCCESS IS ABOUT
A HIGHER LINE MENTALITY

by

Robert Stevenson

SEEKING EXCELLENCE PUBLISHING

Library of Congress Control Number: 2015911019

Raise Your Line: Success is About a Higher Line Mentality
By Robert Stevenson

ISBN 978-0-9654765-5-3   Hardcover
ISBN 978-0-9654765-6-0   E-book

Manufactured in the United States of America

Cover: Design by Damonza

Printed in the United States by BookMasters, Inc.

1 2 3 4 5 6 7 8 9 10

This book is dedicated to
my wife, Annie, and my son Tyler,
who gave up a great deal of the time
we could have been together
so I could have the freedom to
think, reflect, and write.

Warning - Disclaimer

The purpose of this book is to educate as well as entertain; to try and help shorten your learning curve so you may obtain the level of success you desire. Every effort has been made to make this book as accurate as possible. When any support material has been used, I have tried to ensure that proper credit be given to the originating author. Unfortunately, I have a slight dilemma in regard to this matter. I have learned not only from my own personal experiences, but from the experiences of others as well. I have attended hundreds of seminars, listened to countless hours of audio tapes and CD's, read innumerable books, articles, magazines, newspapers and periodicals over the last 30 years from some of the greatest business people, speakers, consultants, and trainers who ever lived.

Therefore, the possibility exists that credit may not be given where it is due, or may even be given to the wrong person. In the event that I have erred, I ask the author to forgive me. My objective has been to be completely fair with everyone and give credit to the correct source.

The author and SEEKING EXCELLENCE, INC. shall have neither liability nor responsibility to any person or entity with respect to any loss or damage caused, or alleged to be caused, directly or indirectly, by the information contained in this book. **If you do not wish to be bound by the above, please don't read any further.**

Permissions:

Personal permission granted by Dave Carroll for the $180 Million Guitar Story

Hachette Book Group – *DELIVERING Happiness* excerpt by Tony Hsieh

ACKNOWLEDGEMENTS

There have been a lot of people involved, either directly or indirectly, in the production on this book. For those indirect folks, thanks for letting me witness, learn, and watch some of life's experiences as a bystander. In many cases, you saved me a great deal of time and pain.

When I finished my first draft, I knew I needed input as to the strengths and weaknesses of the book. The feedback needed to be direct, to the point, no holds barred; I'd rather be criticized by those who know me and care about me than total strangers. I am so fortunate to have not only some great friends, but also friends who have extremely successful careers in diverse backgrounds; from an investment banker, to a Six Sigma/ Lean manufacturing expert, CPA, attorney, teacher, several sales experts and management consultants, business technology expert, two marketing gurus, communication expert, five successful business owners, three mothers with successful business careers, talent agent, and two authorities in merger and acquisitions of large privately held companies … are just some of the titles and positions held by those I enlisted to help me in this project.

I need to give special thanks to Lisa Warren for addressing any editing questions I have and Lisa Coleman, Susan Andreone, Dennis Mandel, Glenn and Valerie Wenzel, Robert "Bob" Esecson, Elliot Price, and Mark Middleton for reviewing the original manuscript and providing me with valuable input, helpful suggestions, candid feedback, and encouragement for this project. Their effort, patience, assistance, and contributions helped to shape the final version of this manuscript and I will be forever thankful to them.

Finally, "much thanks" must be given to my wife Ann and son Tyler, who have become my sounding boards in all that I write. In very simple terms, this book would not have been written without their help; they both played major consultative roles in the development of this book. They have always been there for me, be it when I needed advice, support, criticism, editing, or prodding, to complete the task at hand. **Their commitment to help me in all that I do, is why I am able to do it.**

TABLE OF CONTENTS

INTRODUCTION

SECTION ONE
THE RIGHT MINDSET FOR RAISING YOUR LINE

SECTION TWO
RAISING YOUR LINE AS A LEADER

SECTION THREE
RAISING YOUR LINE AS A COMPANY

SECTION FOUR
RAISING YOUR LINE PERSONALLY

INTRODUCTION

There are certain times in our business and personal lives that we have to make important decisions that will have a huge impact on our future. These **"defining moments"** or **"critical choices"** are the difference between clarity or confusion, misery or joy, success or failure. A few years ago I was the recipient of some rather profound commentary on life. It didn't come to me via some world renowned scholar or teacher; it was casually presented to me by my son Tyler, who at the time was a 21 year-old college student. We were talking about his first few years away at college and I asked him how he goes about making important decisions. He thought for a moment and then said: (I am paraphrasing to the best of my memory) …

"Dad, to me, life is like a line. It can be a straight horizontal line from birth to death, where you don't do anything but basically exist, so there is nothing to cause the line to go up (representing you did something good) …or … causing it to go down (representing you did something bad).

I understand there will be times that my line is flat, which is okay, because you need to take some breaks, vacations, and just relax. I decided my important decisions in life should be based on what makes my line go up. If I study hard and get an 'A' on tests, the line goes up. I see kids doing some really stupid things in college which does nothing to help their line go up … so I don't do them. I am all about making my line as high as I can. So, when I have to make a decision about doing something or not doing something, I think about my line. It helps making a decision so much easier."

Yes, I would say that was some rather profound commentary on life. Complicated just got simple. Confusing just got clear. Indecisiveness just turned into action. **It's all about a higher line mentality.** The same is true in business. When choosing what course to chart, what actions to take, what decisions to make, always do what is necessary so your results are depicted with a higher line.

I decided to write this book based on that concept. I wanted to share as many thoughts, suggestions, and ideas that would help anyone who reads my book be able to **"Raise Their Line"** both on a business and personal basis. That is my commitment to you. If you will apply the suggestions I put forth in this book, you will find it almost impossible to not see YOUR LINE RISING.

It is a simple concept. If you are in the stock market, your success is depicted by a plotted line rising higher and higher as your stock price goes up. If you are a business owner or in management you understand that you want your profits to go up, and that again is depicted with a line on the financial chart going up. My book will be addressing many different lines we encounter in our life both on a personal and professional level.

When I decided on the title for my book I did some research on the word "line." I had no idea there were so many words that have "line" in them … that have a great deal to do with being successful. Let me give you a few examples:

DISCIPLINE - discipline and success go hand in hand. You cannot have one without the other.

STREAMLINE - The successful companies today are doing everything they can to streamline operations. Complicated policies, procedures, rules and regulations are being simplified, replaced, or deleted. Subtraction *(simplifying)* is the exercise of genius … addition *(complicating)* is the exercise of fools … so streamline your operations and your life every chance you get.

DEADLINE - A goal without a deadline is just a wish, so it is important to set deadlines. But, also understand that a missed deadline is more than a disappointment, it is a statement to your client or boss that you can't be counted on.

ONLINE - Being online can be a useful tool for productivity, but it can also be a terrible distraction to productivity if something else catches your attention … so be careful and stay focused on the task at hand.

GUIDELINE - If it was important enough to establish a guideline, then it should be followed.

BOTTOM-LINE - Companies that don't make a profit will eventually fail. It is not how much money a company takes in (revenue) that will make it successful... it's all about profitability. To sustain success, you need to always control your bottom-line.

FRONTLINE - The problem with so many companies today is those making the decisions are so far removed or have been away from the frontline for so long that they haven't a clue what the true consequences of their decisions are until it's too late. If you want to be successful, then you need to stay as close to the frontline as possible. Get out from behind your desk and get on the frontline to see what is really going on in your company.

FLATLINE – A flatline is an electrical time sequence measurement that shows no activity and therefore shows a flat line instead of a moving one. Many people would immediately associate the term to an electrocardiogram, where the heart shows no electrical activity, or a possibly an electroencephalogram, in which the brain shows no electrical activity. In business, it is a very distinctive way of saying an idea, project, plan, scheme, or strategy is dead. It is time to move on to something else because nothing will bring it back to life.

LAUGH-LINE - While you are doing all of this, it is important for you to keep your sense-of-humor and have some fun. Any wrinkle I have on my face caused by my laughing or smiling is a welcomed wrinkle. As far as I'm concerned, laugh-lines are signs you are living a happy life.

LIFELINE - You have no idea how long or short your lifeline is, so make the most of the time you have. Keep asking yourself … *"Is what I am doing taking me where I want to go?"* Your lifeline is a finite amount of time … there are no "do-overs" or recouping of moments lost... so make the most of the moments you have.

SIDELINE - The sideline is not where you want to be. Get in the game. Learn the necessary skills and have the courage to be a player.

D RAISE YOUR LINE

To paraphrase former President Theodore Roosevelt:

The credit belongs to the person who is actually in the arena,

whose face is marred by dust and sweat and blood;

who strives valiantly; who errs, who comes short again and again,

because there is no effort without error and shortcoming;

but who does actually strive to do the deeds; ...

who at the best knows in the end the triumph of high achievement,

and who at the worst, if they fail, at least fails while daring greatly,

so that their place shall never be with those cold and timid souls

who neither know victory nor defeat.

I will be addressing all of these lines in one manner or another throughout my book. Remember, this is all about raising your line(s) on your limited <u>TIMELINE</u>. We all need to pay close attention to how we are handling the LINES in our life.

Over the last two decades I have interviewed over 10,000 employees, managers and senior executives in over 250 industries gathering research to help me prepare programs for my speaking engagements. This book is a compilation of that research, along with all the things I have learned in my over 30 years in business. So understand, this is not just me telling you the things I am suggesting work. These ideas come from people who have lived these experiences, not just studied them. You can shorten your learning curve and advance both personally and professionally by applying proven practices others have developed.

The poem I wrote on the next page is the *"guideline"* I used to decide what went into my book. Each chapter and page has the sole purpose to help you RAISE YOUR LINE(s). Let the title of the poem serve as your mantra for future decisions you make. In everything you do, every decision you make, I believe you should always strive to **RAISE YOUR LINE**.

A Higher Line Mentality

A small fragment upon an endless line represents the time I have on earth.
My line may be short or long and it starts upon my birth.
My line can be uneventful, a dull and boring straight line,
or it can rise, and rise again, marking good decisions on my timeline.

At first my decisions are made for me, a child has little to decide.
But as I grow and come of age, my decisions will mark my ride.
Right decisions make my line rise up, a direction I always want to go.
Wrong decisions make my line go down, a path I hope my line never shows.

It is I who makes my line rise or fall, by the decisions I make each day.
My choices will define who I am, by what I attempt, do and say.
So when choices have to be made, that will affect the path of my line,
I will simply choose what makes it rise, hopefully each and every time.

There is no need to complicate my decisions, choices, or acts.
I will let my line guide me, once I know the facts.
I will learn from my mistakes that cause my line to dip down.
I will benefit from my errors and turn my line around.

Now as I travel on my line, an undetermined time for me,
I will do all that I can, to be the best that I can be.
The time will come when I am gone and all that is left is my line.
To make it stand out from all the rest, I must keep it rising all the time.

SUCCESS IN LIFE AND BUSINESS
IS ALL ABOUT A HIGHER LINE MENTALITY

Throughout my book, I will be emphasizing points which I think are extremely important to your success, by placing them in a box entitled **"LINE RAISER."** I have done so to give you easy reference to those *critical points* after reading my book. So, by simply flipping through the pages you will be able to quickly find those points/suggestions I feel you should give more attention to, so you can RAISE YOUR LINE.

So, let's get started!

SECTION 1

The Right Mindset for Raising Your Line

CHAPTER 1
REALISTIC OPTIMIST

A "Realist" is a person who views things as they really are. An "Optimist" is a person who expects a favorable outcome. I think to be successful on both a personal and professional level you need to be a **REALISTIC OPTIMIST:** *a person who takes in full account the reality of any situation and then using the* **THE POWER OF OPTIMISM***, creates the energy and commitment necessary to achieve higher levels of performance or strives to find an effective solution.* The reason why I decided to make this the first chapter of my book is because I believe everything we do and every decision we make, both personally and professionally, need to be approached as a Realistic Optimist. Not sometimes, occasionally, sparingly … do it all the time. So, from this point forward, read my book knowing that I wrote it based on that premise.

I am the eternal optimist; just ask my wife. She will tell you I can watch a movie that is *really bad* and the whole time I am thinking it will get better, the plot will improve, the actors will become better actors, and the ending will be great. As a *motivational* business speaker for over 20 years, I have preached the power of optimism and how you should incorporate it in everything you do. But, I am also a businessperson who has owned several companies, worked with over 2,500 other companies, **and interviewed over 10,000 employees, managers and senior executives in over 250 industries,** so I understand where optimism needs to stop and realties must be addressed.

Former President John F. Kennedy would assign a person at each cabinet meeting **to take the opposite view** of what was being proposed, even if they agreed with it. Their job was to serve as **THE CONTRARIAN** and try and shoot holes in the plan, find the weak points or destroy it altogether, if they could. He felt if a plan, idea, or suggestion couldn't stand up to their tough questions, the plan sure wouldn't stand up to the real world when they tried to implement it. He knew, because he was the president, many times people would publicly agree with him, even when they really didn't agree. He understood that the only way to get real answers was to take the *fear of reprisal* out of the picture. If you are having meetings and everyone is agreeing with you, then you don't need to have any more meetings. Disagreements are healthy; President Kennedy insisted on them.

Zappos, the internet shoe selling company, who went from zero to $1 billion in sales in 10 years, changed its own business plan four times before making it big. They were able to address the outcomes of decisions they had made and then adjusted their business plan to deal with those realities. A&P, who had over 16,000 stores, didn't pay attention to their customers' ever-changing demands *(the true realities of their marketplace);* they didn't adjust their business plan accordingly, and they now have about 300 stores left.

It is great to be optimistic; I want to be surrounded by people who know we can get it done. But, I also want to be around people who will face reality and change when necessary; then get it done. ***That's the way we've always done it,*** and it works for delivering great service, having great attitudes, being timely and efficient; those are all critical to your success. But, when your market changes, when customer demands change … when technologies change … when nature alters plans with its destructive forces … when health issues arise … you have got to be realistic about the facts facing you and react accordingly. You might want to be an NBA basketball player starting at the center position, but if you are 5'5" tall, it isn't going to happen. GET REAL with yourself. The odds are not in your favor. What odds? It isn't going to happen. Deal with it and move on.

Let me give you a very personal example of having to deal with the REALITY of the situation. When our son, Tyler, was 9 years old he was diagnosed with type 1 diabetes. The reality of the situation on that day was, there is no cure for this disease and he would be insulin dependent for the rest of his life. Optimism will not make his disease go away. Optimism would only help us deal with the situation. The REALITY of the situation was our life had immediately changed, plans would have to be altered and procedures would have to be set in place if we were going to be able to cope with this disease and keep our son as healthy as possible. Ignoring the disease would only end up making him seriously ill and jeopardize his life.

Our OPTIMISTIC attitudes helped us deal, handle, cope and control his *moment by moment* fight to stay healthy, but the REALITY was then and unfortunately still is as of today … he will never be cured. We will forever be OPTIMISTIC about finding a cure for diabetes, but we know first-hand, that only by staying diligent and REALISTICALLY facing the facts and doing what is necessary every day, can we hold off the damage to Tyler's body that diabetes can cause.

I have heard the phrase, ***"Get Real"*** countless times. To be successful in life and business, I believe that phrase needs to be your paramount mindset in everything you do. Dig for the facts, verify the data, question all concerns … simply *"Get Real."* Regardless if it is business or personal, you always need to be realistic about the facts facing you. Ignoring reality will only cause more pain in the end. **The most critical step for solving any problem is to first *fully understand the problem*; sugar coating the issue, denying what is really there, declining to accept the facts, is a sure path to disaster. *"Get Real!"*** Once you understand what you are up against, then you can apply your optimism to resolve, tweak, adjust, make accommodations or simply eliminate the issue and move on to GETTING THINGS DONE.

Please understand that this book is not about the exceptions to the rule, it's about REALITY. There will always be people who overcame incredible odds or went against conventional wisdom, knowledge, or data, and still succeeded. I will be addressing different business and personal performance issues in a realistic manner. My objective is to help you make better decisions in the future so you can **RAISE YOUR LINE.** If you intend to be successful in all walks of life, then it is critical you deal with issues both realistically and optimistically.

I have said it countless times in my speeches, but it is worth repeating; ***if you don't like change, you are going to hate extinction.*** If you are going to stay ahead of your competition then address **the real issues, ask the tough questions and be ready to change**. Whether you are leading employees, coaching or teaching children, commanding a platoon of soldiers, making decisions for your family or for yourself ... approach everything realistically with an optimistic attitude.

> # LINE RAISER:
> To survive in this ever-changing marketplace,
> to deal successfully with whatever
> life or business throws at you,
> I suggest you become a ... REALISTIC OPTIMIST.

"A PESSIMIST SEES THE DIFFICULTY IN EVERY OPPORTUNITY; AN OPTIMIST SEES THE OPPORTUNITY IN EVERY DIFFICULTY."

SIR WINSTON CHURCHILL

If you want to **Raise Your Line** then start approaching everything as a

Realistic Optimist.

CHAPTER 2
Success is Never Final

The reality of it all is there will always be technological change, global competition, the uncertainty of stock markets, fluctuations of commodity prices, and unnecessary government regulations. Disorder, uncertainty, even occasional chaos will confront you on a regular basis. There is no certainty that key employees, associates, vendors, and customers are going to stay with you, nor is there any certainty of what the future holds for you. But, the great news among the certainty of all this uncertainty is that some companies still survive. Not only do they survive, they literally thrive while other companies underperform, fall or fail to the everyday pressures of the marketplace.

If you are going to be successful you will have to navigate through all the chaos and uncertainty. Great leaders accept the instability and uncertainty as just part of the game. I call business a game because if you know how to play it you will win, but if you don't know how to play it, you will lose. Two hundred and thirty of the Fortune 500 companies that existed in 1980 are gone. Go back 10 more years and that number jumps to 74%. **The simple point to understand is if you do what you've always done, you'll be gone.** Loyal clients are hard to find. Your competition is just waiting for you to drop the ball so they can scoop it right up and run with it. Your customers, bosses, and associates are all thinking, *"Don't tell me what you did for me yesterday, tell me what you are going to do for me tomorrow."* If you want to be successful you might want to consider living by the following suggestion:

LINE RAISER:
Wake up every morning knowing
your success for today will not be based on
yesterday's victories nor tomorrow's dreams.
You must deliver TODAY!

One of the big problems I see with companies today is that they don't really know what differentiates them from their competition. If I was conducting a **Strategic Planning Session** for your organization today, the first thing I would ask you is - **"What does it take to be great in your industry?"** I would then ask - **"Where are you excelling ... where are you meeting the standard ... where are you the weakest?"**

You've got to understand your strengths, especially those that differentiate you from you competitors. But, you better fully understand where you need work. Years ago, *The Harvard Business Review* stated, **"1 in 24 customers complain, the other 23 just go somewhere else."** When your clients leave, they are a great deal harder to get back than they ever were to get the first time. They left because you did something wrong and upset them; overcoming an upset attitude is far harder than getting someone to do business with you the first time. To get someone to become a loyal customer you need to develop TRUST, CONFIDENCE, and RAPPORT. When you upset the customer you have damaged all three.

LINE RAISER:

Ask your customers this question: *In a perfect world, if we could provide you with perfect service ... where do you feel we are falling short?*

Many companies fail because of arrogance. I think we would all be hard pressed to find anything good about being arrogant. I do not like dealing with arrogant people, or companies who have the pretentions of superior importance. I don't want an arrogant boss, friend, or associate, and I sure don't want to deal with an arrogant company. You know the type; *we're so big and wonderful ... you are lucky we are even talking to you.*

Motorola grew from $5 billion to $27 billion in annual revenues in just one decade. In the early 90's they were seen as one of the most visionary companies in the world. They were known for their willingness to experiment and especially for their methods of self-improvement. They are the folks who pioneered "Six Sigma" quality programs and anticipated future opportunities a decade away.

Somewhere in all this enormous growth and incredible success their culture shifted from that of "humility" their founder had instilled in the organization into "arrogance." They had the **arrogance** to dismiss the threat of "Digital Cellular Technology" believing that since they had a 50% market share, they could "control" the consumer. They had the **arrogance** to start dictating to their distributors/retailers that 75% of all phones they offered to the public "must" be Motorola. In 2001 Motorola had 147,000 employees, by the end of 2003 they had laid off over 60,000 of them and their stock price had plummeted.

At one time IBM had an 82% world-wide market share. In the 80's they took the top spot on Fortune Magazine's **Most Admired Corporation** four years in a row. In The 90's they had $15 billion in cumulative loses over a three year period, and their market capitalization plummeted from $105 billion to $32 billion; they almost didn't survive. Andy Grove, former CEO of Intel once said:

"Only the paranoid survive.
Paranoids believe someone or some force
is out to get them."

Unfortunately, Kodak didn't heed Mr. Grove's comment. A company who invented the Brownie Camera, Instamatic Camera, and the Digital Camera … whose camera was the first to be used on the moon … who had over 1,100 digital camera patents … who at one time had a 90% world-wide market share in photographic film, 64,000 employees, $31 billion in sales, and was in business for over 100 years … went bankrupt. It would be very hard to be concerned about survival with those kind of business stats, but statistics are about what you've done, not what you need to be doing. Kodak for some reason couldn't accept the changing of film to digital in time to save itself. How ironic, how sad, how strange it must be to know you invented the product that caused you to go bankrupt.

In 1995 Circuit City was touted as one of the best companies in the world, having grown more than 20% per year for a decade. They had hundreds of stores and billions in sales, but in November of 2008 they filed for bankruptcy. The stories go on and on; Rubbermaid, Arthur Andersen, Eastern Airlines, Barings Bank, Bethlehem Steel, Enron, Sunbeam Products, Worldcom, Countrywide Financial, Lehman Brothers, Wachovia, Washington Mutual, Blockbuster, Citigroup, Scott Paper and Zenith all let success and sometimes their arrogance, get the best of them. There is an ancient saying:

"One benefits when being humble with fellows and loses when being superior."

Don't assume because you have been in business for 40, 50, or 100 years, or you have an enormous market share that you will keep it, because just when you start thinking you are good, someone else will come along that's better. Never forget what the great Sam Walton said:

"There is only one boss, the customer, and they can fire everybody in the company ... from the Chairman on down ... simply by spending their money somewhere else."

Bloomberg-BusinessWeek magazine, in their article *The Living Company*, stated the average life expectancy of a multinational corporation-Fortune 500 company or its equivalent is 40 years. All great companies once started from humble beginnings, and if they are not careful, they can end up there. **Arrogance is not a virtue, humility is.** Treat everyone special ... because the *"not-so-important-folks"* of today may someday become important ... and they will remember how you treated them. Be fearful of start-up companies because they are hungry and they know they have to beat you with their resourcefulness, not their resources.

Never forget the power of staying PARANOID, and the need for staying humble. You have to prove yourself every year, month, day, hour, minute, and moment. Use the attitude of ***From Hero to Zero*** in everything you do. Understand you have to prove yourself every time; future success does not come to those who rest on their laurels. Always be alert to the possibility of being surpassed, beaten, or outdone. You might have won the game or beat out your competitor yesterday and that's great. Feel good about it! But never lose sight of the fact that they lost and they are now regrouping and getting ready to come at you again. They are rethinking their weak points as well as searching for yours. They are putting together a NEW GAME PLAN to take you down so you better not relax. You better be reloading, preparing, tweaking, and improving because "THEY" are. Never forget what Andy Grove said: ***"Only the paranoid survive. Paranoids believe someone or some force is out to get them;"*** someone or some force is the "THEY" I am talking about.

LINE RAISER:
Always remember ...
Success is NEVER final.

CHAPTER 3
HUMBLE BEGINNINGS

• In the early 1960's, Phillip Knight and his college track coach, William Bowerman, sold imported Japanese sneakers from the backend of a station wagon. They invested $1,000 in start-up costs to get their company off and running.

• In 1907, two teenagers from Seattle began a message-and-parcel delivery service for local merchants. The total investment to get their company started was $100.

• With $900, Tom Monaghan and his brother bought a small pizzeria in 1960 and expanded their company using a simple strategy: locate their stores near college campuses or military bases and deliver their pizza within 30 minutes of receiving an order. Tom Monaghan didn't finish college, but as he would note, he stayed long enough to learn that college kids eat a lot.

• In 1933, with $923 of their own money and $5,000 that they borrowed, two brothers with no business experience, rented a warehouse in Modesto, California, and launched their business. Not only were they lacking business experience, they learned their new chosen profession, wine-making, by studying pamphlets at the local library.

• An old, white-haired man drove around the country, giving out samples to people, of what he had cooked in the back of his station wagon. He wanted to show people just how good his fried specialty tasted.

• Michael started his company in his college dorm room and ended up dropping out of college. Harvard college drop-out Bill and his high school friend Paul, moved into an Albuquerque hotel room, started a little computer software company and went bankrupt. Restarted it again, with a slightly different name, and the rest is history.

Today might not be going so well for you … and you or your company might be facing challenges or competition that seems to be overwhelming. I think it is safe to say …

Nike
United Parcel Service
Domino's Pizza
E & J Gallo Winery
Kentucky Fried Chicken
Dell Computer
Microsoft

all felt the same way numerous times. Success comes to those who will persist, fight, challenge, and change when times get tough. Nothing worthwhile ever comes easy. If those great companies can come from such humble beginnings and make it work … so can you. The key word in all of this is "WORK."

LINE RAISER:
Create a culture of humble respect for your success and be forever mindful that each day you must prove yourself again.

The original **McDonald's** was opened by two brothers in California back in 1937. In 1954, Ray Kroc discovered the small burger restaurant and the rest is hamburger history. **Starbucks** started in 1971 founded by three former students from the University of San Francisco … two teachers and a writer. **Apple** started in a garage to sell personal computer kits. **Google** was started in 1995 by a couple of college computer geeks also working out of their garage, and they forever changed the way we retrieve information. Humble beginnings … I rest my case.

CHAPTER 4
HOW'S THAT WORKING FOR YOU?

There is a man who comes to the gym where I workout who is at least 50 pounds overweight. He started coming about a year ago and he looks exactly the same size as he did then. If his goal was to lose some weight, then he better re-evaluate what he is doing, because **it isn't working.** In all aspects of life and business I think it is important to ask ourselves, *"How is that working for me / us / the company?"* Sometimes, you may want to even enlist the advice of a friend, associate, or consultant and ask them how they feel about what you are doing. Asking the question is the easy part; listening to the answer and then doing something about it, is where it gets tough.

Years ago, Rubbermaid set out to invent a new product every day, 7 days per week, 365 days per year. Fortune magazine once wrote that Rubbermaid was more innovative than 3M, Intel, and Apple; now that is impressive. Then Rubbermaid started choking on over a 1,000 new products in less than 36 months. Innovation became more important than filling orders on time, overhead expenses, or cost controls. They ended up closing 9 plants and laid-off over 1,100 employees before Newell Corporation came in to buy (rescue) the company.

I had a mentor who once told me,

"Rob, I don't care how hard you work … I care how smart you work. Results are what counts."

Rubbermaid was working hard, putting in time, money, and effort while at the same time destroying their company. *How was that working for them?* The REALITY of the SITUATION … it wasn't working for them. Innovation for the sake of innovation doesn't insure success. Hard work, effort, and activity don't insure success. Those are all great things to have as long as they help you/me/us/ the company reach our goals.

Insanity has been defined as ...

Doing the same thing, the same way, and expecting a different outcome.

As I stated in my introduction, A&P at one point was the largest food retailer in the world (over 16,000 stores) and just couldn't accept that what they were doing wasn't working anymore. They now have 3% of their stores still operating. Ames Department Stores had over 700 stores and $5.3 billion is sales, Montgomery Wards had over 500 stores and $6.6 billion in sales, Service Merchandise had over 400 stores and $4 billion in sales and these companies are now defunct; something definitely didn't work for them.

Remember what I said in the previous chapter: *create a culture of humble respect for your success and be forever mindful that each day you must prove yourself again.* Instill in yourself and your people that if you aren't getting better every day ... you will lose. Markets move, power shifts, new inventions and technology change dominance, so always feel vulnerable and then OVER-PREPARE. To stay ahead of your competition you need to start thinking - *If you were competing against yourself, how would you beat you ... and then fix it.*

LINE RAISER:
LOOK FOR THE WEAK P'S
**Look for weak POINTS, weak PEOPLE,
weak PROCEDURES,
weak POLICIES,
and either fix them or get rid of them.**

Change is to business as what oxygen is to life. In life – you can either breathe or die. In business - you can either keep changing or die. Change is **the** constant in all aspects of life. Successful people, companies, organizations and associations all **_deal with it_** – losers don't. One of the big problems we all face is that most people seem to have a negative reaction when you introduce the word "Change" into a sentence.

- *"We need to change our methods"*
- *"We need to change markets"*
- *"We need to change software"*
- *"We need to change managers"*
- *"We need to change the schedule"*

Everyone starts thinking, *"Oh great. I've got to learn something new, or find new customers, or study how to use new software, or get used to a new manager, or alter my family schedule to help the company."* Seldom is the word *"change"* received in a positive way, so, rather than use a word which puts most everyone on the defensive, try and rephrase what your change is really all about. To me ...

Change is the Relentless Pursuit of Excellence.

You aren't changing to get worse, make things harder, confuse customers, or confound employees. You are simply trying to GET BETTER at whatever it is you are trying to do. Most people don't have a problem with ...

Getting Better
Making Things Easier
Beating The Competition
Becoming More Profitable
Protecting Their Future Employment

The **Realistic Optimist** ... Leader / Manager / Boss ... looks at the facts, analyzes results, and asks for lots of opinions before making any changes. If you raise your price and sales instantly plummet, it doesn't take a marketing genius to determine you might want to re-think your new pricing structure. If a competitor moves into your market place and sales instantly plummet, then you better rethink everything you've been doing.   Your happy customers might give the competitor a try, but if you are really delivering the best service, product selection, and attitude along with a fair price … they will be back.

But, we are still at a CRITICAL POINT when it comes to *how's that working for you.* It is one thing to know it isn't working; in fact, that is half the battle to fixing the problem. If you don't know **"it's broken"** you aren't going to be looking for ways to fix it; so, congratulations on realizing it is broken. But, now that you know it isn't working, the next question is … *What* isn't working? I will address how to handle what isn't working later on in the book.

This section of my book is about having the right mindset to **Raise Your Line.** If you get anything from my entire book, I hope it is this statement:

Before Asking Others to Change, Change You First.

Several years ago I was correcting my son about something annoying he was doing. I was trying to explain to him why he shouldn't do it and that other people might also find it annoying. Tyler and I have a pretty open relationship and I try to encourage him to speak freely to me on any subject. So, after I corrected him, he asked me what he should do if I did something that annoyed him. I said that he should let me know. Tyler then proceeded to mimic a couple of things I do that annoy him. My wife, Annie, happened to be in the room and I thought she was going to break a rib, because she was laughing so hard at Tyler's depiction of a couple of my annoying habits. He kept going and Annie kept laughing.

There I sat in all my glory, receiving a mirror image of a couple of my annoying habits from my son. What should I say now … how should I react to this telling depiction of myself? Do I take umbrage because my son *(who was 15-years-old at the time)* was correcting me? And don't forget, my wife was not coming to my defense; she was just about falling on the floor, laughing so hard.

So what did I do? I started laughing, too. Tyler really wasn't trying to be mean. He had hit that nail right on the head, and that nail was me. Annie was probably thrilled with what Tyler had done. I am sure they were both hoping I would heed his words and correct my bad habits.

I have shared the following statement in my programs countless times: ***"Before asking others to change, change you first."*** We all, especially me, need to follow that advice. So, the next time the *"Tyler" in your life* makes a suggestion about something you could improve upon, change, or quit doing, before taking offense, give it some thought. Their suggestion could make you better and that is what this book is all about … getting better … RAISING YOUR LINE!

I think a tough book to buy would be ***Success for Dummies***. You walk up to the check-out counter and the person at the register looks at the title and then looks at you … they don't have to say a word … you know what they are thinking. Now, you could follow their look and say, ***"The book is for someone else."*** Yeah, right. I am sure they will buy that. I did a little research on book titles *(I own none of these)* and came up with a short list of other odd book titles.

Self-Esteem for Losers

You Mean I'm not Lazy, Stupid or Crazy?

You are Worthless
Depressing Nuggets of Wisdom Sure to Ruin Your Day

Right now you are probably asking yourself, what is my point to all of this? Other than the fact that there are some seriously questionable book titles out there, my real point is this**; why do we care so much about what other people think?** Your success is about, ***you, because of you,*** and has nothing to do with what some stranger thinks about you.

What I think is important is GETTING BETTER, LEARNING MORE, and REFINING OUR SKILLS. I happen to own the book ***Success for Dummies*** and I found it helpful. I probably won't ever again see the person who sold me the book, and even if I do, I am the one who got better because of the book I read; not him. I also read several other strangely titled books, such as … ***Purple Cow,***

A Whack On the Side of the Head, Who Moved My Cheese, The Complete Idiot's Guide to Managing Stress, Fish, Nuts, and *Eat the Frog.* I benefitted from reading each one of those books.

Remember, no one came into this world with all the answers. Successful people are always looking to improve and reading is one of the quickest ways to do that. You can greatly shorten your learning curve and reduce your mistakes (disappointments) by reading about the experiences of others. I try not to let a day go by that I don't spend some time trying to improve myself.

LINE RAISER:
Make it a practice every day to read or listen to something that will enhance "YOU."

YOU ARE ALL YOU'VE GOT,
SO THE BETTER YOU GET
THE BETTER FOR YOU.

The last point I want to make about having the right mind-set to raise your line is to quit taking things for granted. When I am in town, I try to go to a local gym and work out as often as I can. It's a great way to start off the day, and I find by going in the morning rather than putting it off until the afternoon, I seem to be able to go more often. **I like going at the same time every day** when the gym has as few people in it as possible. That way I can get my workout in without having to make it a social hour.

I share the *"same time every day"* information with you because of what happens after I leave the gym. As I am driving home, I see the same man taking his dog out for a walk. His dog looks excited to be out, pulling hard on the leash with his tail wagging. We have all seen people countless times taking their dog out for a walk. There is nothing unusual or really special about that, unless you add that the man is in a motorized wheelchair. We all take so many things for granted until we lose them. A simple walk around the park with your dog becomes an extremely difficult task when you have to do it in a motorized wheel chair. When my son Tyler tore his ACL (Anterior Cruciate Ligament) in his right knee, a simple shower became a major ordeal. Every once in a while we need to step back and reassess our attitude, look at our lives in a different perspective, and **start appreciating what we have.**

When I look at the man in the wheelchair, he becomes my inspiration for having a great day. I am certain he would give anything to be able to simply go to the gym as I had. I never gave it much thought until I saw him. Sometimes life sends us a little signal and we are just too busy to see it.

LINE RAISER:
Start appreciating what you have because
**you will never know when it can be gone in an instant.
Life just sent you a little signal; are you paying attention?**

SECTION 2

Raising Your Line As a Leader

CHAPTER 5
"Leader" An Earned Title – Not Given

Many people profess to have *Leadership Ability,* but few people truly possess it. They read the books, listen to the tapes or DVD's, go to the seminars, and then pronounce themselves Leaders. They use words like *empowerment, total quality management, excellence, vision, commitment,* and in the same breath, want to take the credit. As James O'Toole, a professor and leadership expert puts it, **"Ninety-five percent of American managers today say the right thing. Five percent actually do it."**

I recently worked with an old friend who had chosen to go with a new company. Having worked with him several times before in other organizations, I had seen his management style in action. It was a sheer delight to watch him operate in a new company and see that he had already been awarded the title of LEADER by his staff. He is a man who respects, understands, directs, motivates, and helps everyone around him … a man who can be given a difficult task and accomplish it while at the same time CARING for all employees and customers. Lao-Tzu, a revered philosopher of ancient China, left us with an excellent explanation of leadership.

> *The superior leader gets things done with little motion.*
> *He imparts instructions not through many words*
> *but through a few deeds.*
> *He keeps informed about everything but interferes hardly at all.*
> *He is a catalyst, and though things would not get done as well*
> *if he weren't there, when they succeed he takes no credit.*
> *And because he takes no credit, credit never leaves him.*

Managers who think they must make people feel stupid, insecure, or scared to get things done will never become great leaders. It is not just how good employees perform when you are there, it is also that they perform well when you are not there; that is the true benchmark of a great leader. Great leaders see the potential in people and cultivate it; they build confidence... not destroy it. Leadership is about helping others, teaching others, supporting others, giving credit to others – **It's about OTHERS – It's not about YOU!** Great leaders never look for fame, accolades, or awards – they dwell on accomplishments and the rest follows.

You will know you are a leader
when you start making the people around you BETTER.

LINE RAISER:

**Start looking for the potential in people and cultivate it.
Do everything you can to build confidence, not destroy it.
Look for what people are doing right and build on it …
rather than find out what they are doing wrong
and berate them.**

CHAPTER 6
Bad Decisions Lead to Mistakes Then Good Judgment

I think sometimes we lose the perspective of where good judgment comes from. We aren't born with good judgment. Some good judgment slowly evolves from the knowledge our parents, teachers, coaches, bosses, and mentors try to share with us. Some good judgment evolves from doing something so many times that we figure out what works best. But often, we unfortunately have to live through a bad experience to gain the knowledge/wisdom.

I read one time that **"Good judgment comes from experience and _a-lotta-that_ comes from bad judgment."** Mistakes are a wonderful source of insight so I think it is important to never let a mistake go to waste. You can't get the mistake back but you sure can learn from it, so you don't do it again. I tell companies that they should keep a list of their mistakes, write down every detail, and then share them with the new employees; this is a great way to reduce the possibility of having the same mistake occur again. You don't want new employees making old mistakes … any mistakes they make should be new ones.

When a mistake is made it is also important to understand that the person didn't mean to do it; **people don't set out to mess-up.** Now, they could have been lazy, not followed the instructions, been in a hurry to meet a deadline, or done something foolish … but doing it INTENTIONALLY is seldom ever the case. Another way to reduce mistakes is to pass along **words-of-wisdom** by sharing tricks, short-cuts, experiences or stories that have helped you become a more qualified, skilled and knowledgeable person. Sometimes those _wise words_ sink in and help to eliminate mistakes from occurring.

Here are a few _words-of-wisdom_
I think you might find helpful.
(the author of each quote is unknown)

> ➤ *Do not corner something that you know is meaner than you*
> ➤ *Words that soak into your ears are whispered ... not yelled*
> ➤ *You cannot unsay a cruel word*
> ➤ *Meanness doesn't just happen overnight*
> ➤ *Remember that silence is sometimes the best answer*
> ➤ *Letting the cat outta the bag is a whole lot easier than putting it back in*

I don't care where I get the knowledge from ... just as long as it helps me. You need to understand that mistakes are not final, nor is failure. If learning is good and making mistakes is all a part of learning ... then I think it is fair to surmise that making mistakes is simply a part of the learning process. Albert Einstein once said ...

*"Anyone who has never made a mistake
has never tried anything new."*

LINE RAISER:
Look at every first-time mistake as a part of the
WISDOM PROCESS
... get over it and learn from it ...

YOUR JUDGMENT JUST IMPROVED

As a leader, you need to take this chapter and internalize it. You have got to understand that people are going to make mistakes and not mean to. When they do mess up, the first thing you should ask yourself is, ***"What have I done to cause them to fail?"*** Many times mistakes were made because the instructions were poorly given or not detailed enough. Never lose sight that the first mistake is a part of the learning process; correct it and move on. If the same mistake happens again by the same person, you now have a process or personnel problem that has to be dealt with.

There will be occasions, as a leader, that you will be **BAFFLED, PERPLEXED,** or **PUZZLED** with how to deal with some situation or problem. I would like to share a short exercise with you, that for many of you reading this book, will have a problem figuring out the answer. Yes, I feel the exercise below will surely challenge your *problem solving* capabilities. I didn't figure it out. I was baffled, perplexed, puzzled, and totally stumped. With that being said, I wish you luck in trying to figure it out, and if you do, BIG KUDOS to you. Here is the exercise/question.

See if you can figure out what these seven words all have in common!

Banana – Dresser – Grammar – Potato – Revive – Uneven – Assess

Study it. Think Hard! You are going to KICK YOURSELF when you discover the answer. No, the answer is not that they all have at least 2 sets of double letters … ***Banana*** kills that because it has 3 "A's", so that isn't the answer. **The answer is at the end of the chapter,** so if you can't figure it out, go read the answer and then come back and read what I have to say about this exercise and why I shared it with you.

My first point about this exercise is sometimes as bosses, managers, or leaders, we don't have the answer. So, get over it and admit it. Great leaders know how to bring the right people together to FIGURE THINGS OUT. One of my clients has a team of people they call ***THE PITS CREW.*** When things are THE PITS, bad, awful, totally messed-up …when things go so wrong and there seems to be no solution to the problem … the ***person-in-charge*** calls corporate and tells them to send in ***THE PITS CREW.*** At that point, they stand aside and turn over control. Now, that doesn't mean that THE PITS CREW won't be calling on them (or anyone on their team) for input, suggestions, ideas, or thoughts … but it does mean that whatever THE PITS CREW figures out will be implemented.

Equally important, if I were putting together a ***Pits Crew,*** you can **_take-it-to-the-bank,_** that my **CREW would be made up of** different talents, skills, backgrounds, ages, and genders. Sometimes a brilliant mind can't see what a less experienced mind can or vice-versa. Sometimes senior management gets stuck in the *"that's the way we've always done it"* mode. Sometimes youth jumps at an answer that a more experienced person has already tried and found it didn't work.

It is absolutely amazing what can be accomplished if people aren't worried about who gets the credit or blame. *THE PITS CREW* is there to find out what caused the problem, fix it and set up procedures so it won't happen again. There are no politics, only remedies. They feed off each other and know that the *"Cure to the Problem"* will come from their cooperation with each other. **Always remember, the first step to solving a problem is admitting you have one.**

Agendas, Egos, Tenure, or Titles
Never Solve a Problem
A Variety of Talents, Insight,
and Cooperation Will.

Here is the answer to the exercise:

In all the words listed,

Banana – Dresser – Grammar – Potato – Revive – Uneven – Assess

If you take the first letter and place it at the end of the word, and then spell the word backwards, it will be the same word.

I told you that you would want to kick yourself
when you read the answer.

CHAPTER 7
The "*Ripple Effect*" Principle

If you drop a pebble into a pond where the water is still, you will see a beautiful circular **"*Ripple*"** motion take place where the stone entered the water. That one pebble sets in motion ripples that will affect the entire body of water. The same thing can happen in life, business, or organizations. One idea, thought, policy, gesture, example, statement, or extra effort can set forth a **"*Ripple Effect*"** that can forever change you, your company or organization for the better.

Several years ago Alcoa Aluminum, the world's leading producer of primary and fabricated aluminum, brought in a new plant manager at one of its many facilities. When driving up to the plant he had been assigned to on his first day in his new position, this new plant manager noticed that all the good parking spots by the front entrance had the names and titles of the so-called "important people" painted on them. **The FIRST thing he did was contact the maintenance department and told them to paint over all the names and titles, his included.** This one decision sent **"*Ripples*"** throughout the entire plant. This new manager instantly sent a message that **everyone is important, every person matters,** and extra effort deserved extra benefits; if you got to work early, then you got a great parking space.

This one decision electrified the plant and had an amazing **"*Ripple Effect.*"** People started showing up early and feeling they really mattered. Attitudes changed, better lines of communication opened up. The new manager wanted everyone to realize that management was there to support employees, increase efficiencies, mentor, advise, and assist ... not demean or scare people. When you are manufacturing a product that involves handling 1220°F molten aluminum, every person is critical to the process. They were all in this together and one gesture by the new manager had just set the tone.

LINE RAISER:
Today, identify one thing you should concentrate on
that will have a positive *"Ripple Effect"*
on you or your company.
The *"Ripple Effect"* Principle can work for anyone out there.

(Here is a personal example of the "Ripple Effect")

These are just a few of the ripples that occur when you **decide to be early**
by leaving 15 minutes earlier than you intended to leave.

1. Reduce your stress
2. Keep you from rushing and possibly making bad decisions
3. Impress people that you showed up early
4. Allow you to network a little before a meeting
5. Shows that you are organized and ready

As a leader your job is to decide on which important things you need to be dealing with and what decisions you can make that will have the most positive *"Ripple Effects"* in your company.

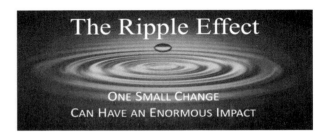

But, as a leader, you are still going to have to deal with the resistance to change. Just as soon as you use the word "CHANGE" the hair will go up on the back of their neck and, in most cases, a defensive attitude will raise its ugly head. So, let's take a look at change another way.

ADJUST VS. CHANGE

Unexpected things happen all the time that we have to deal with, whether we want to or not. We can adjust to the circumstances or resist them. I find the people who adjust are a great deal more successful than the ones who don't. It is one thing to be stubborn to your convictions, it is entirely different thing to be unaccepting to the new circumstances that have just occurred. Instead of looking at things under the painful guise of **"Having to Change,"** I think it is more effective to say, **"It's time to adjust."**

I would say it is definitely TIME TO ADJUST when your company decides to let you go. Oh, they can say it in so many different ways; they can tell you they are retrenching, downsizing, rightsizing, re-purposing or re-aligning staff. I had one client call it a "RIF." For those of you who aren't familiar with this acronym... it stands for ***"Reduction in Force."*** I guess you might say that is a nice way to tell people, if there is such a way, they have been laid off. But in your eyes, you see it as being canned, kicked to the curb, booted out, terminated, shown the door, sacked ... or in the simplest of terms ... FIRED. I heard one person say they had been issued their "DCM" notice, which stands for ***"Don't Come Monday."***

Whatever a company wants to call being "laid-off," the reality is you now have to ADJUST to this new situation. I really prefer using the word ADJUST rather than CHANGE, because it seems easier, in context, to do.

> ➢ The weather changes and you ADJUST what you are wearing.
> ➢ The economy changes and you ADJUST your spending habits.
> ➢ Traffic is bad and you ADJUST your route.
> ➢ Production is down so you must investigate the cause and ADJUST.
> ➢ Your health changes and you ADJUST your exercise and eating habits.
> ➢ Your boss changes and you ADJUST to their style of management.
> ➢ You have a newborn baby and you ADJUST your sleeping habits.
> ➢ You get married and you ADJUST from an "I" to a "We" way of thinking.
> ➢ Sales are down so you must ADJUST advertising or prospecting activity.

In business you have to ADJUST to competition, technology, economic issues, healthcare issues, rising expenses, changes in media advertising, changing demographics of customers, and availability of workforce ... to name just a few.

LINE RAISER:

Instead of using that painful word "CHANGE,"
may I suggest you start looking at approaching things with an
ADJUSTMENT mentality.

People have a real tendency to resist change,
but they do seem more accepting of
ADJUSTING to the circumstances.

Sometimes it is just the perspective of how we are going to address a situation/problem that will help people buy into doing what is necessary to fix it. Most of the time you don't have to change everything to fix a problem; you just need to make some ADJUSTMENTS. Which would you rather hear,

"You have to CHANGE what you did."
... or ...
*"With a few minor adjustments,
what you did is going to work great?"*

Our world is constantly changing ... so your life is in a constant state of adjustment. Always remember, there are things you can't change so you must ADJUST or you will not succeed. As a leader, you have to understand that great **"Ripple Effects"** can sometimes occur with a few minor adjustments. You don't have to always create radical changes when things aren't going the way you want them to.

SUCCESSFUL LEADERS KNOW THAT IF THEY AREN'T REACHING THEIR GOALS IT IS TIME TO ADJUST THEIR ACTIONS.

CHAPTER 8
Barn Movers

Great leaders understand the power in teamwork. They also understand that all ideas should be given full consideration, even if they seem a bit far-fetched. The following story is a wonderful example of how, a seemingly crazy idea turned into an incredible reality though the power of teamwork.

In 1981, Donna and Herman Ostry bought a farm in the small town of Bruno, Nebraska, about 60 miles outside of Omaha. The farm came with a big barn that had been built back in the 1920's, and also had a nice little creek that flowed through their property. The creek was both a blessing and a problem for the Ostrys. It was great to have readily available water for their farm animals, but it also flooded a lot during heavy rains. The barn floor seemed to always be wet and muddy, and then in 1988 they had a huge flood where the water rose about 30 inches up the side of the barn walls.

The Ostrys desperately needed to move the barn to higher ground but the cost to contract with a company that has both the capability and equipment to move a barn of this size was prohibitive. One night sitting around the dinner table, Herman Ostry commented that if he had enough people he could pick the barn up and move it to higher ground. Everyone laughed off the comment as silly ... everyone except his son Mike.

I wonder if "young" Mike knew that people scoffed at the idea of traveling 30 miles per hour on a railroad car. People actually thought that traveling that fast would stop the circulation of the blood. I wonder if "young" Mike knew that Eli Whitney was laughed at when he showed his first cotton gin, that Thomas Edison had to install his electric light free of charge in an office building before anyone would look at it, that Westinghouse was considered a fool for suggesting you could stop a train with wind, or that Samuel Morse had to plead before 10 Congresses before they would even look at his telegraph *(which revolutionized communication)*. Knowing those facts certainly would have helped to convince "young" Mike that his idea may not be as ridiculous as most people would think it is. OR, maybe "young" Mike just thought ... **_WHY NOT_** ... and then he set out to figure a way to make his dad's statement a reality.

Young, inexperienced, doesn't-know-any-better Mike did some calculations and figured out that the barn weighed about 17,000 pounds. He then figured out that he could design a steel grid system that he could place under the barn that would weigh another 3,000 pounds. So, the total weight that would need to be lifted was 10 tons. When you think of that amount of weight to be moved, you usually think of a giant crane ... not a whole bunch of people. But, Mike figured if he could gather up about 350 people, they would all need to only be able to lift approximately 50 pounds each.

Mike presented his calculations to his dad and they both thought it would work. Mike and his dad got a little lucky on the timing to present their idea to their small town. Nebraska was getting ready to celebrate its centennial, and the town of Bruno had put together a committee of townspeople to decide on different things to do for the celebration. Mike and his dad convinced the town to make the barn moving a part of the celebration. The word got out and over 4,000 people from 11 states witnessed the event. Here is the YouTube link to the actual event.

http://youtu.be/o83W0gj_CRE

A little before 11 a.m. on July 30th, 1988, in front of the local television cameras, 344 people moved the barn 143 feet up a gentle slope to its new foundation. **_All in all_**, it took 3 minutes to move the barn. So, the next time somebody hits you with an idea that you think is silly or maybe even impossible ... think again, and **never discount the POWER of TEAMWORK.** Re-live this idea again in your head. Someone in a meeting says:

"Let's move a 17,000 pound barn,
143 feet, up a slope,
and do it in less than 3 minutes,
using no machinery."

Now that idea sounds pretty nuts, ridiculous, stupid, impossible, and far-fetched to me. But a need, a desire, a creative mind, a well-designed plan and a giant team, **ALL WORKING TOGETHER**, made it happen!

TEAMWORK REALLY MAKES THE DREAM WORK
(anonymous)

LINE RAISER:
It is your job as a leader to keep an open mind
and understand there might be several different ways
to accomplish the same task.
If conventional methods are not available to you,
then perhaps you should consider the unconventional.

CHAPTER 9
It's Okay to Change Your Mind

What is so wrong with changing your mind? Nothing! If you made a decision that didn't work out ... then *change your mind*. If your life or business isn't going the way you want it to go ... then *change your mind* and go a different direction. No matter *what is going on in your life or what has gone on in your life*, in every situation, regardless of the circumstances, you have the ability to alter the way you feel about it by *allowing yourself* to *change your mind.*

So many people worry, fret, cry, or stress-out over things they shouldn't. You have an incredible power available to you ... anytime you want it ... that can make you feel better, and put you on track to a better day; *the ability (power) of changing your mind.*

When you *change your mind* about anything, it transforms how you now perceive it. It puts you in a better frame of mind and you now start seeing how you can make things work rather than dwell in the debilitating mood of self-defeat; *changing your mind becomes and energizing force.* Making a decision to alter your course becomes a catalyst for emerging ideas. Your mind wants a direction, a course, a decision, and when you give it that clarity, it rewards you with new hope, inspiration, and energy. *You quit floundering in your indecision and flourish in your new direction.*

Remember the shoe company Zappos, who changed their business plan four times; they learned from what was going on and not working, and then *changed their mind,* changed their direction and changed their outcome. In management, you might make a decision that didn't work out so well or was poorly received. You can use that bad decision to your benefit by simply saying you have reconsidered your decision because of the input you have heard from everyone, *changed your mind,* and have decided to go in a new direction.

Not every decision you make will be right. Realize that and understand *smart people and effective managers are the ones who are willing to CHANGE THEIR MIND and move on.* Stubbornness and inflexibility can kill a company and a career.

LINE RAISER:

Change Your Mind

Hit the Reset Button
Start Over From a More Informed Position
New Beginnings Bring on New Energy,
New Ideas and New Results

CHAPTER 10
The Carpet People

The other day I had the opportunity to hear four managers from large companies give 15 minute presentations about things their companies were doing to improve productivity, morale, and communication. The first speaker got my attention instantly when he said his people were always complaining about the "CARPET PEOPLE."

He had just been promoted as the new boss of one of the largest manufacturing facilities his company operated in the United States. A couple of days after his arrival he heard the term "CARPET PEOPLE." He said that he didn't want to look like an idiot not knowing what the term stood for, so he kept his mouth shut for a while, hoping he would eventually figure it out; but to no avail. He finally pulled one of his employees aside and asked what the term meant.

That employee said the term "CARPET PEOPLE" was directed at management. The only place in their enormous manufacturing facility that had carpet on the floor was in the offices where management worked. If a question had to be answered, they had to go talk to the "CARPET PEOPLE." No supervisors had offices on the main manufacturing floor ... so production employees would always have to waste time and go find the "CARPET PEOPLE" to get an answer.

**It was not meant as an endearing term ... I can assure you.
It was an US vs. THEM mentality.**

He said that once he understood the term and why it was being used, he immediately changed things. He didn't want production stopping on the factory floor because his people had to go find a "CARPET PERSON" ... so he had those offices moved ... **to front and center on the factory floor** ... where production managers could be quickly located; it should also be noted ... they had NO CARPET in their offices on the factory floor.

The next three speakers played right off of this story and used other non-endearing terms for their management people ... such as the "Shiny Shoes," the "White Coats," and the "Suits." In a lot of companies, the moment employees see *these people* heading their way, they want to run, hide, look busy, and they know whatever they do they don't want to get in their way, strike up a conversation, make a suggestion, and they definitely don't ask them a question. Speak only when spoken to and refer anything they ask to your direct supervisor if at all possible.

There are some managers out there who love being the boss, being seen as the Carpet Person, wielding a mighty *"whip of authority"* ... with a *"my way or the highway"* mentality. Some even believe the best way to deal with morale problems is just fire anyone who complains. I learned years ago that effective managers help people get better and should be looked on as a "knowledge base" for employees to call on anytime to help evaluate, correct, adjust, or address any tough situation they can't handle. If employees fear their supervisors, managers, or bosses ... productivity and morale is sure to suffer. It has also been proven through countless studies, that employee turn-over will also become a problem.

If management is asking for teamwork, collaboration, synergy, unity, cooperation, looking for camaraderie, wanting employee input, and seeking suggestions and new ideas, then management needs to pay attention to how they are being perceived. A hierarchy, top down, status based, authority riddled, pecking order doesn't seem to be very conducive to creating any of the things I just mentioned.

NOTE:

One of the managers who spoke,
said they decided that if management
was to walk on the factory floor,
then they needed to wear the same thing
all employees were wearing ...
so they came up with a corporate polo style shirt
(all the same color) that everyone wore.

LINE RAISER:

Take note of the things you are doing
that separates management from everyone else
and try to minimize it as much as possible.

There is a big gap of dissension
between the **"Carpet People"** and having true teamwork.

You Don't Mandate Unity
You Cultivate It

CHAPTER 11
B. O. S. S.

Are you the type of **BOSS** who brightens the meeting when … **you leave**? Are you the type of **BOSS** when people see you coming … **they hide**? Are you the type of **BOSS** when you call, text or e-mail an employee they … **get scared**? I sent out a "Tweet" the other day about being a boss and a lot of folks retweeted it. Evidently, my tweet struck a nerve, so I decided to expand upon my short message. This is what I sent out …

Being a __BOSS__ should stand for Be-Open-Sensible-Supportive. It should not stand for Be-Oppressive-Stubborn-Superior.

The simple definition of a **"BOSS"** is a person of authority over employees. The problem is that many employees would describe their boss with one or more of the following terms:

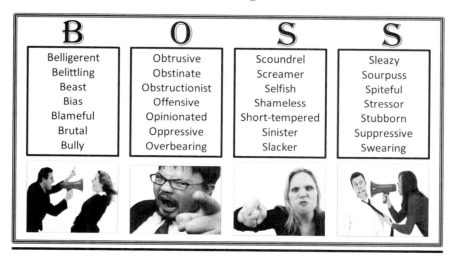

B	O	S	S
Belligerent	Obtrusive	Scoundrel	Sleazy
Belittling	Obstinate	Screamer	Sourpuss
Beast	Obstructionist	Selfish	Spiteful
Bias	Offensive	Shameless	Stressor
Blameful	Opinionated	Short-tempered	Stubborn
Brutal	Oppressive	Sinister	Suppressive
Bully	Overbearing	Slacker	Swearing

So many **BOSSES** have the attitude … I am the Sheriff in town and it's my way or the highway. Well, *Yep-ee-ki-yah,* sheriff … that attitude won't endear you to your employees. If you profess to be a **BOSS** or someday want to be, let me give you some scary statistics to think about. A Gallup poll of more than 1 million employed U.S. workers concluded that **the #1 reason people quit their jobs is a**

BAD BOSS or immediate supervisor. Researcher and author Robert Sutton discovered that no matter what the occupation, roughly 75% of the workforce listed their immediate supervisor/boss as the most stressful part of their job.

According to Gallup, people leave BOSSES, not companies ... so in the end, turnover is mostly a **BOSS** issue. The **BOSSES** from hell are creating active disengagement costing U.S. companies an estimated $450 billion to $550 billion annually, stated Jim Clifton, the C.E.O. and chairman of Gallup. It seems crazy to spend so much money properly training employees only to run them off with a **BAD BOSS**. Excellent rewards, stimulating work environments, health insurance, and other perks will not make a difference to the people stuck with **BAD BOSSES**.

Common complaints about **BAD BOSSES** are they fail to keep promises, fail to give credit when credit is due, make negative comments about subordinates to other employees or managers, invade privacy, they are uncaring and arrogant, they use fear tactics, and they blame others to cover up their own personal mistakes. It should also be noted, there is NO EXCUSE for sexual harassment or discrimination of any kind. *I learned a long time ago it is better to create an environment where people WANT to deliver for you rather than HAVE to deliver.*

As I have already pointed out, most of the time the words, *"I Quit!"* are caused by the boss. Here are a few, **unfortunately common thoughts**, of some bosses out there:

THE BOSS:

> ➤ *"Don't think of me as your boss, think of me as a friend who is never wrong!"*

> ➤ *"When I want your opinion, I'll ask for it."*

> ➤ *"We don't pay you to think. We pay you to work."*

> ➤ *"You want recognition? We recognize you every time you get a paycheck."*

> ➤ *"Your job is what I say it is."*

> *"You're lucky to even have a job."*

> *"I don't know what it is that you need to improve, but something is definitely wrong and you should work on fixing it."*

And, here are a few, **unfortunately common thoughts**, of some employees out there:

THE EMPLOYEE:

> *"The only way I would ever work here again is if the world was coming to an end ... because every day working here feels like an eternity."*

> *"You can't pay me enough to ever want to work here again."*

> *"You treat us all the same – AWFUL ... I QUIT."*

I was recently talking to staffing industry expert, Daniel Abramson, about why people leave companies. I met him when he was the president of an international staffing firm with 120 offices. He now has his own firm (www.staffdynamics.biz) and is helping companies in their hiring and retention practices.

I wanted his input on the troublesome problem of why "Qualified, Talented, and Needed" employees leave companies, especially when it costs so much money to find, hire and train them. The last three words of his first statement to me were very disconcerting. He first stated the obvious, "There are several reasons why good people quit" ... but then added ... "MOST ARE PREVENTABLE." OUCH! **Here are his 5 TOP REASONS why employees leave firms:**

1) Lack of corporate compatibility and fit
2) Lack of appreciation by management
3) Lack of support from inside staff
4) Limited advancement & personal growth opportunities
5) Money & Compensation issues

He also mentioned that *"People don't quit their company, they generally quit their boss,"* and *"Too much emphasis is placed on the technical aspects of the job and not the soft people skills."* I suggest if you are having a problem with a particular employee, you might want to move them to a different department, reporting to a different boss before firing someone that you have invested so much money in; some people just aren't meant to work with each other. And while you are doing your reassignments, make sure you give both the manager and employee some help with their soft skills. *(Soft skills, sometimes known as "people skills," are personal attributes that enhance an individual's interactions, job performance and career prospects: they would include optimism, common sense, responsibility, a sense of humor, integrity, time-management, motivation, empathy, leadership, communication, good manners, sociability, and the ability to teach … to name a few)* Refining everyone's soft skills can cause a huge boost in productivity for any company.

It costs a lot of money to replace an employee; some experts say it can cost up to 20% of a worker's salary to replace them. With that amount of money at stake … what can a company do to reduce those expenses and use that money in a more beneficial way? Where should a company start if they want to keep their top employees?

According to the U.S. Department of Labor, 46% of employees leave their job because they did not feel appreciated. I would be starting there. It doesn't cost a dime to tell people *they are doing a great job, you really appreciate their contribution, this company is a better place because of them, I don't know what I would do without you, you made it happen — thanks for all your effort;* it's free, effective, and smart!

Compliments Cost Nothing
It is Unspoken Praise That is Costly

Simply stated:
There is Power in Appreciation

The pioneering psychologist and philosopher William James once said, ***"The deepest human need is the need to be appreciated."*** Remember, the U.S. Department of Labor stated that 46% of the employees who voluntarily quit their jobs ***do so because they didn't feel appreciated.***

We all want to feel appreciated not for just a job well done, but for showing up every day, for being on time, for being proactive, for lending a helping hand, for having a smile on our face. It seems most managers today get so caught up in the day-to-day pressures of meeting quotas, goals, and objectives, that they forget to compliment, thank, and appreciate all the folks around them who make it possible for them to meet all those quotas, goals and objectives.

It doesn't cost a dime to appreciate an employee - but it costs a great deal of money not to. If a qualified employee leaves, you now have separation processing costs, hiring costs, training costs, lost productivity and possibly lost revenue. *Keep Employees, Inc. (a leading employee retention consultancy)* puts a dollar amount on the costs of losing a productive employee:

FOR HOURLY EMPLOYEES

0.25 to 0.50   times their annual wages plus benefits

FOR MIDDLE MANAGERS

1.00 to 1.50   times their annual salary plus benefits

FOR TOP MANAGEMENT

3.00 to 5.00   times their annual salary plus benefits

Remember the Gallup poll that concluded that the number one reason people quit their jobs is a "bad boss" or immediate supervisor. Common "bad boss" behaviors (in case you need a reminder) are bullying, harassment, discrimination, and lack of respect. I would assert that a boss who made an effort to appreciate and compliment their employees would seldom, if ever, be described with any of those oppressive behaviors. To me it is just plain bad business to lose an employee who is qualified, doing their job, and contributing to the company's success, because you neglected to go out of your way to tell them they are doing a good job.

If you want to increase productivity, morale, efficiency, effectiveness, resourcefulness, competency, and teamwork *then start making the effort of appreciating all those around you.* If corporate and personal success interests you, then start showing some interest and appreciation to your employees and associates.

When you start showing people you care about them and appreciate their efforts, you will be amazed at the benefits it will bring. But understand one important point. **This is no one time affair. Done properly... it is a way of life!**

LINE RAISER:

So, for you **BOSSES** out there ...
or those hoping to become a **BOSS** ...
strive to make **BOSS** stand for:

BOSS..... Believe in your people... Open-minded... Sensible... Sincere
BOSS..... Big-hearted... Objective... Savvy... Spirited
BOSS..... Bold... Observant... Scrappy... Supportive
BOSS..... Brave... Optimistic... Self-controlled... Sympathetic

And if you strive to be all of those traits ...
those who work for you
WILL be SUCCESSFUL and so will you.

CHAPTER 12
The Amazing Power of Four Words

Some say the four most powerful words in coaching are, *"I believe in you."* I think we need to expand that to teaching, mentoring, management, leadership, parenting, and relationships. What a wonderful thing to tell somebody, *"I believe in you."* Think of how it made you feel when it was last said to you. Oh, there's the problem ... are you having trouble remembering when someone last said it to you? That is truly a shame, because the words are SO POWERFUL and have a way to motivate, inspire, and encourage us all. But the flip side of this is, when was the last time you told somebody those words? Are you having trouble remembering when? That is a shame as well.

In our personal lives, so many times we take for granted the ones we love the most and give them the fewest compliments. Oh sure, they know we love them, they know we think they are really talented, they know we appreciate the little and big things they do for us, they know we feel we can always count on them ... sure ... they know. Right? **A compliment not given is no compliment at all.** Inspiring words not shared are not inspiring at all. Don't assume people know how they are doing, when your mouth never utters a word.

In our business lives, we also take people for granted. *Remember, the U.S. Department of Labor found that 46% of the people who quit their jobs, did so, because they didn't feel appreciated.* We spent the money to find them and train them, but we can't utter a few words every so often to let them know they are doing a good job. The words are free ... they cost you nothing ... but not saying them can end up costing you a lot.

I have had bad teachers and good teachers, bad coaches, and good coaches and bad bosses along with some good bosses. I can't ever remember any **BAD** teacher, coach, or boss being a positive person. NOT ONE. But, I can remember that my good teachers, coaches and bosses all had a positive side to them. I wanted to do more for them and not let them down. I would never want to disappointment them because THEY BELIEVED IN ME and told me so.

What a wonderful thing it would be to have someone say ...

"Because of you, I succeeded."
"Because of you, I didn't give up!"

We all need affirmation; some of us need it more than others. If you want people to produce more, raise their level of competence, perform at a higher level, and deliver more than expected, then follow my next suggestion.

LINE RAISER:

Let the following four word phrases become part of your every day life. Great teachers, managers, coaches, and bosses (leaders) all know they should ...

Show them the way	Help them keep trying	Make them feel special
Be there for them	Help them learn more	Inspire them to succeed
Prepare them to win	Show faith in them	Be a confidence builder

---

You will be amazed what a positive effect the phrases *"I believe in you!"* or *"You can do this!"* can have on people. If you don't believe me, just give it a try. It sure can't hurt to try and it costs you nothing to do it ... but it could be costing a lot to stay silent.

All GREATNESS REQUIRES CONFIDENCE
All CONFIDENCE REQUIRES HELP

I just don't understand why some people in positions of authority think that being mean, condescending, and/or cruel are effective ways to get the most out of people. I have, unfortunately, run across numerous bosses, managers, and teachers who are just plain mean. I guess some folks feel that when they are given a position of authority, or the title of *Supervisor, Vice President, District Manager*, etc., that they are now entitled to say and do whatever they want because they have *"the authority"* … they have *"the title."* Their associates, employees, or students are now below them and they can treat them as such.

Depending on what industry you are in, it costs somewhere between $5,000 to $75,000 to properly train an employee. I have had several clients tell me they have spent a great deal more. So why in the world would you spend all this time, effort, and money to then have some manager rip into an employee and start to drive them away from your organization? You also might want to heed the old wise tale, **"As you treat your employees, they will in turn treat your customers."**

I believe words like respect, fair, concern, help, assist, facilitate, teach, show, lead, and care, are far more effective than push, yell, scream, force, scare, intimidate, bully, threaten, harass, and drive. I have always tried to follow the simple rule of …

"Praise in Public, Criticize in Private."

I would also suggest that if you have to criticize an employee, try and find something they are doing right, and talk about that for a few moments before sending them out to deal with fellow employees or customers.

I asked my son, Tyler, if he could only pick one teacher from all the teachers he had from kindergarten through grad school (over 50 teachers), who would his favorite teacher be? With very little hesitation Tyler said, Mr. Martin. Mr. Martin was his middle-school history teacher. He was an African-American teacher, retired military, a couple of years away from retirement, who had total control of his class. He demanded a lot out of his students and Tyler had to work hard in his class, but he still liked him. I asked Tyler why Mr. Martin was his favorite and he said, **"Well Dad, he was fair. He told us he wouldn't try and trick us on tests. If we listened in class, took good notes and then studied the notes we would do well."** He then added, **"And then after a test, if there was any time left in class, we would do some fun things. He likes to laugh and make others laugh."** Let's see what we have here:

A tough, demanding, old school, teacher ...
being respected and liked by a teenage student.
Who would have ever thought that possible?

I don't like mean people; never have, and never will. I don't want to be associated with them, work for them, or be taught by them. And, if I have a choice, I will go somewhere else.

LINE RAISER:

Quit thinking you have to yell, scream, force, scare, intimidate, bully, or threaten employees to be an effective manager and leader.

Always ... *"Praise in Public, Criticize in Private."*

And more importantly,
respect everyone, treat them fairly, be concerned about them, and help, assist, facilitate, teach, show, lead, and care about them.

CHAPTER 13
Developing Talent

How much time per year do you think a person should spend perfecting their profession? Should they work 99% of the time and study 1%? Should they study 2%, 5% or 10% of that time trying to learn how to become more proficient at their job? **According to the American Society for Training and Development (ASTD) the average number of hours spent in a classroom by an American worker is 26.3 hours per year.**

If you had 2 weeks' vacation per year and added another week for holidays, that would give you 49 workweeks. Based on a 40-hour workweek, you would have 1,960 work hours per year. According to the ASTD, 26.3 of those hours are spent in the classroom. That would mean the average American worker spends less than 1.5% of their workday perfecting their profession. To look at these numbers in simpler terms ... **on average, American workers spend 6.5 minutes per day developing their talent.**

If you are an employee of a company reading this article please don't rely on your company to make you better at your profession. I suggest if you want to catapult yourself to the top of your company/profession, you spend a minimum of 30 minutes per day studying / reading / learning ways to get better at what you do for a living.

If you are a manager or company owner reading this article, I suggest you make the investment to enhance the talent level of your people. Make sure they have the necessary time allotted to them so they can study ways to perfect their profession.

Jack Welch, the former CEO of General Electric, spent over 70% of his time on finding and developing talent. During Mr. Welch's tenure as CEO of GE he increased its market capitalization by $400 billion, making it the world's most valuable corporation. McKinsey & Company, one of the foremost consulting firms in the world stated; *"Mr. Welch was arguably the best talent developer in the past century to occupy a corner office in America, or perhaps the world."*

To become a great leader you need to be aware of *The Pygmalion Effect;* **a phenomenon in which the greater the expectation placed upon people, the better they will perform.** The work of Robert Rosenthal and Lenore Jacobson (1968), among others, shows that teacher expectations influence student performance. Positive expectations influence performance positively, and negative expectations influence performance negatively. This phenomenon has been proven over and over again in scientific studies, yet so few people, parents, coaches, trainers, managers, and leaders take advantage of it.

The research that has been conducted since Rosenthal and Jacobson's original study has determined that *The Pygmalion Effect* applies to all kinds of settings, from sports teams to the military to the corporate workplace. Therefore, the great news about *The Pygmalion Effect* is you can elevate the achievement of others if you practice a few simple steps. There is no magic involved, **just an attitude of having higher expectations for those who work for you (*or with you)* will lead to better results.** Here are a few things you can do to start making *The Pygmalion Effect* work for you.

■ SUPERSTARS can handle more so we tend to put more on them with an encouraging statement of, *"I wouldn't be giving you this, but I know you can handle it."* Your attitude of expecting promising results for handling a heavier work load or a more difficult task helps them achieve it. They are actually thinking, *"Well, if my (parent, boss, coach or teacher) thinks I can do it ... I guess I can."*

■ If you think you have a SUPERSTAR working for you, you will have an open mind to their suggestions or feedback and respond to any of their questions in a helpful manner, rather than a frustrated one.

■ When you know you have a SUPERSTAR working for you ... you unconsciously create a friendly working environment that has less stress, because you know they can get the job done. You walk by and give an encouraging smile, a nod of approval, and sometimes stop and give an approving comment for whatever it is they are doing. Your attitude towards them, treating them with respect and expecting they will succeed at whatever they are doing, will cause them to do better. *So, start treating people as SUPERSTARS* and watch how they will start performing better.

■ We have a tendency to give more personal feedback on the performance of a SUPERSTAR and use them as examples to others. Complimenting someone in the presence of others is a huge boost to any ones ego. **Always remember to "Spread Praise in Public" whenever possible.**

Smiles, positive feedback, encouragement, public and private praise, pats *on the back*, approving head nods, reassurance, support, better explanations, better instructions, being open and receptive are all things that come from you. *Remember the quote ... "If you want others to change, change you first."* The key to making *The Pygmalion Effect* work for you, your organization, company, team, or students, is a change in your behavior.

German writer, philosopher, and politician, Johann Wolfgang von Goethe, once said ...

> *"If you treat an individual as he is,*
> *he will remain how he is.*
> *But if you treat him as if*
> *he were what he ought to be and could be,*
> *he will become what he ought to be and could be."*

Goethe also said ...

> *"The way you see people is the way you treat them,*
> *and the way you treat them is what they become."*

Could elevating the performance of others be as simple as *The Pygmalion Effect* suggests? Why not give it a try. It sure can't hurt.

LINE RAISER:

If you Want to *Pump-Up* Your Profits
You Need to *Pump-Up* Your People

While you are "Pumping-Up" your profits and people it is critical that <u>YOU</u> remember to stay "Up." It is simple to make the statement that as a leader you need to stay positive, optimistic, and motivated; it is an entirely different thing to actually do it. **This book is all about Raising Your Line. You need to constantly remember the direction you want your line going – UP.**

So, let's talk about UP for a moment. Your words can build people up and your words can tear people down. Words can ruin careers, and the right words can motivate people to accomplish things they never thought possible. Being a professional speaker, I am always searching for the right words that will produce the best results in getting my message across. From time to time, in my search for the right words to use in my programs, I come across a word that seems to have many meanings and uses. One such word is "UP."

Some of the definitions of "UP" are… *to, toward, or in a more elevated position: at or to a higher place: to a higher station, condition, or rank: concluded; ended; finished; terminated: going on or happening; taking place; occurring.* But, these definitions really don't do justice to the word. The word "UP" has a treasure trove of meanings and uses. You can catch-up, clean-up, build-up, shake-up, follow-up, look-up, and change-up. You can be up-rooted, up-ended, up-right, up-front, up-lifting, and up-dated. You better not screw-up, crack-up, cover-up, blow-up, or throw-up … and sometimes you have to put-up or shut-up.

As a leader you need to get-up-and-running, be up to the task, fire-up your people, follow-up with customers, shape-up employees, speed-up processes, tune-up bad procedures, line-up great new employees, back-up the computer, hook-up with new customers, brush-up your presentation, and check-up on everything. You don't need to cover-up mistakes, stir-up problems, hold-up progress, make-up excuses, and especially not up-stage your boss.

And while we are on the subject of "UP" … may I also suggest you always try and be a stand-up person who tries to up-lift people's spirits while building-up their confidence. I think I've gotten my point across and opened UP your eyes as to how important it is for you to stay UP. Remember, your people are always watching you; **YOU** are the person responsible for setting the tone, creating the right working environment where they can excel.

Raising Your/Their Line is "UP" to you.

Robert W. Woodruff was the president of The Coca-Cola Company from 1923 thru 1954 and then served on their Board of Directors for another thirty years. Coca-Cola hired him when they were in financial difficulty, and he turned the company around and helped to make it an international powerhouse with one of the top three most recognized brands in the world.

Mr. Woodruff was an amazing leader with a straight-forward and fair management style. He decided one day to put in simple terms his strategy on Human Relations; this is what he had to say:

The five most important words in the English language:
"I am proud of you"

The four most important words:
"What is your opinion"

The three most important words:
"If you please"

The two most important words:
"Thank you"

The least important word:
"I"

LINE RAISER:

Make those 15 words from Mr. Woodruff
part of your everyday
Leader Vocabulary
and let others sing your praises.

Make the investment, spend the time, and reap the benefits.

Great Leaders know the more they
Raise The Line
of their employees,
the more they will raise the
Profit-Line
of their company.

CHAPTER 14
Leadership Secret – Laughter

Laughter is a POSITIVE STIMULANT to Profits. If you want your profits up, then it is time to incorporate humor into your work environment. I recently did a speaking engagement for a company, and in my research interviewing process, several people shared with me some very disturbing comments about their working environment. I simply asked the question, *"What do you do for fun at your company?"* I received comments like …

> *"We don't have time for fun."*
> *"I can't remember the last time we did anything fun."*
> *"Fun – we don't do anything fun."*
> *"I think we had a picnic last year."*

Due to the pressures to produce more in less hours and the ever-increasing pressure of competition, in too many companies today, humor and laughter have virtually disappeared. If you want to boost productivity, then figure out ways to create a fun, happy work environment, and most importantly, make people laugh. One study conducted by Canadian financial institutions, discovered that **managers who used humor often, also had the highest level of employee performance.** If you are still not convinced that laughter is something that you should strive to create in your workplace, then here are a few more facts that might help.

► Laughter can defuse anger and anxiety as well as keep you focused and alert
► Laughter is contagious and irresistible and therefore, spreads within your organization
► Laughter boosts your energy, diminishes pain
► Laughter protects you from the damaging effects of stress
► Laughter adds joy and zest to life, eases fear, and improves your mood

► Laughter enhances resilience, strengthens relationships, and enhances teamwork

► Laughter helps you keep a positive, optimistic outlook through difficult situations

It is important to make time for fun activities at work: e.g. bowling night, miniature golfing, karaoke, watch clips from a funny movie or TV show, share a good joke or a funny story, check out your bookstore's humor section and bring some books to a meeting to share, host a game show night or lunch break with associates, ask people, *"What's the funniest thing that ever happened to you,"* include humorous quotes or pictures in communications, use *improv* games as icebreakers and stress busters, organize group activities outside of work that are fun, have impromptu theme days as well as caption contests, and/or have a dress-up day or different theme costume dress-up days and give out awards for best costumes.

LINE RAISER:

Have a meeting strictly devoted to figuring out ways
to have FUN at your company and then do them.
Never forget that laughter is a
POSITIVE STIMULANT to profits.

Humor/Laughter is a powerful tool but you must be careful how you use it. Victor Borge once said ... *"Laughter is the closest distance between two people."* That is one reason why I like to use a lot of humor in my presentations. Laughter is a powerful force, that when properly harnessed, can create positive attitudes, emotions, and outcomes. But, as a professional speaker, one of the hardest things for me to find are funny, good, clean, polite, non-offensive jokes. Another thing I have to be careful about is the joke being perceived to be funny by the audience. If I tell a joke and they don't laugh, that's not good. If I tell several jokes and they don't laugh, I just turned the audience off and any effectiveness I hoped to achieve in my speech has been greatly diminished.

So, I try and inject humor into my programs through the use of stories. I may think the story is humorous, but if my audience doesn't … that's okay, because I was just telling a story. But, if my audience finds the story humorous, I have energized them and sparked their attention span. If they find the story humorous and it makes a point they can remember … I have hit a home run.

I feel humor is a wonderful business asset. People like to laugh. It makes them feel better, it makes them trust you and it helps make people more receptive to your ideas. By using humor, you can pull people into a comfortable surrounding and they will start to enjoy themselves and listen. I have a couple of simple rules about using jokes and humorous stories. **First,** I think if you offend one person in the audience with your humor, you lose … so … you have to be really selective in your use of material. **Secondly**, never, under any circumstance, make fun of someone else in the audience. If there is anyone to be laughed at, that would only be me.

You can also use humor to make a serious point as General Norman Schwarzkopf did when he was asked at a press conference about the military ability of Saddam Hussein. The General said …

"As far as Saddam Hussein being a great military strategist, he is neither a strategist, nor is he schooled in the operational arts, nor is he a tactician, nor is he a general, nor is he a soldier. Other than that, he's a great military man."

The press corps erupted in laughter. What a powerful and humorous response which endeared the General to his troops, the world press and Americans but more importantly, made his message more memorable.

So, the next time you want to be better received you might want to include some levity into your presentation. Here are some statements that could be perceived as funny, but at the same time have a message.

Everybody has the right to be stupid … some people are just abusing the privilege.

*To err is human – to blame it on someone else
shows management potential.*

*Knowledge is knowing a tomato is a fruit.
Wisdom is not putting it in a fruit salad.*

… the quotes are by Dave Berry, Unknown Author,
and Miles Kington respectively.

LINE RAISER:
Lighten-up
Laugh
Share the Humor

Laughter can help people thrive during change,
remain creative under pressure,
work more effectively, and
stay healthier in the process.

**Make sure laughter is part of your
every day work environment and watch
ALL YOUR LINES RISE!**

CHAPTER 15
Looking for Credit, Accolades, Praise, or Honor

There is a word in the English language that can have an immediate and negative effect on many people when used. It is a simple, little, one-letter word, but boy can it turn people off when they hear it. That damaging word is "I." *I did this ... I did that ... I was the one who thought of that ... I made it happen ... I decided.*

By using the word "I" you are really congratulating yourself. You are making a public statement explaining just how pleased you are with yourself and what "YOU" accomplished. Before making a self-congratulatory statement, you might want to consider just how many other people were involved; people who had something to do with what was accomplished. By taking sole credit for the accomplishment, you just upset everyone involved in the task.

There is an old Chinese proverb which states, *"You cannot propel yourself forward by patting yourself on the back."* Credit, Accolades, Praise, or Honor should be given ... not taken. They are only meaningful, deemed special, when extolled by others. You can't prove your superiority by personally telling the world how great you are, but you can prove your lack of confidence.

Many people confuse confidence with egotism. Egotism is a tremendous weakness. If you ask someone if they can do something and they say, *"Absolutely" ... "Yes" ... "Not a problem,"* those are not egotistical responses, they are responses of confidence. But, if they go around boasting they did it ... that is where egotism kicks in.

LINE RAISER:
When something has been accomplished and you want
to announce it to the world, using words like
"they" or "them" are far more powerful and endearing
to all those listening to what is being said.

The moment YOU put the word "I" into the accomplishment is the moment YOU hurt YOUR reputation and stature.

Anatomically speaking, it is quite difficult to take your hand and pat yourself on the back, but it is simple to point to others, give them credit, and pat them on the back; *remember that* the next time you start to use the word "I." You can never go wrong in singing the praises of others, but singing your own praises will never become a top hit song.

Great Leaders Understand that Credit, Accolades, Praise, or Honor only have VALUE when GIVEN by others.

CHAPTER 16
A Culture of Ownership

I have a client who is an extremely large freight company with an amazing delivery-on-time ratio of over 99%. But, it is not just getting the merchandise there on time that makes them so good, it's getting it there on-time and undamaged. They concentrate on getting their people to **think like an owner**, to try and recognize problems and take ownership of the problem rather than leave the problem for someone else to fix. (*In most cases, fixing a problem after-the-fact, costs more and results in a seriously upset customer.*)

So, they have instilled a **Culture of Ownership** throughout their organization by showing their people how and when ownership of a problem should take place and the costs associated with no one doing so. They put together a short film for a training conference as a case study, using an actual client event. This "event" could have been corrected countless times had anyone taken ownership; but no one did. Here is a quick look at what the film identified.

The freight company's salesperson finally convinced the client, who manufactured golf carts, to give them a try at shipping their carts around the country; an order for three truck loads. Did the salesperson go check how the golf carts were packaged? **No.** *He just turned in the order to operations and moved on to the next customer.*

Operations sent over three trucks to pick up the golf carts. Did those three drivers check to make sure the golf carts were packaged correctly so they wouldn't get damaged in transit? **No.** *They just loaded up the golf carts and took them back to the main terminal. Then they proceeded to off-load the golf carts, so they could be placed on individual trucks to be shipped out the next day.*

Did anyone in the terminal (over a hundred people), who walked by the golf carts while they were sitting on the terminal floor, recognize that they were packaged incorrectly and would easily be damaged in transit? **No.**

Not one person took ownership of the problem. No one was looking out for the company, or for that matter the customer. Did the golf carts arrive safely? **No.** *Every one of them was damaged. Did the freight company pay the claim?* **YES!** *If one person had taken ownership, thousands of dollars would have been saved, along with keeping a HAPPY customer.*

If your company is going to be successful you need to get your people thinking like an owner; taking ownership of any issue that could negatively affect your company or the customer. The short film by the freight company said it all. *__Great Leaders__* realize that if they intend to *__Raise The Lines__* of efficiency, productivity, and profits, it is critical they *Create a Culture of Ownership.*

Now let's carry this concept a little further into developing the overall "Corporate Culture" of your company. The dictionary defines "Corporate Culture" as the distinctive ethos (the fundamental character or spirit) of an organization that influences the level of formality, loyalty, and general behavior of its employees. It includes the philosophy, shared values, traditions, customs, and behavior of a corporation, that together constitute the unique style and policies of a company. Wow! That was a mouthful to swallow all at once.

LINE RAISER:

A simple way to determine what is your company's
current corporate culture ... is to select a
random sampling of people within your organization
and ask them to explain
what they believe to be your corporate culture.

You may want to take a seat when you hear what they have to say. In most cases their words will astound you. If by chance you hear similar responses from most everyone that mirror the culture you were hoping to create, then get excited, because you have just hit a home run. Your training is working, your leadership is working, and your communication channels are working. BUT, if your people have a glazed look in their eyes, wondering what answer you are looking for or if their responses are extremely dissimilar, then you have a problem.

A Gallup poll of the American workplace showed that 72% of American workers aren't engaged in their jobs.

The J.M. Smucker Company has everyone who is hired memorize their printed corporate culture creed entitled, **"Why We Are – Who We Are."** Smucker's wants their people engaged. They believe their "culture" is the cornerstone to their success and must be proactively protected by instilling the creed in each and every employee.

How is your "Corporate Culture" doing?

I believe the J.M. Smucker Company is an excellent role model to follow for teaching anyone how to successfully run a business today. Founded in 1897 making apple butter, this company now employs over 4,700 employees and is doing over $5.6 billion in sales. Tim and Richard Smucker are the Co-CEOs for the J.M. Smucker Company and they believe they serve 6 constituents:

"The Consumer, The Retailer, Our Employees, Our Suppliers, Our Communities, and Our Shareholders.

We believe if we take care of the first five, the sixth will be automatically be taken care of."

They live and work by the creed, *You Will Reap What You Sow.* Here are their rules for achieving success in business:

- Let the Golden Rule guide every decision.
- Don't have secret strategies ...
  make sure everyone knows the strategy and knows their role.
- Have a culture that promises people a better tomorrow
  based on their good work.
- Don't be content; you're responsible for making things better.
- Doubt your own infallibility.
- Have faith. Believe in a higher force.
- Don't do what you know only for material rewards ...
  be called to your life's work and have a purpose.
- Laugh and have a sense of humor.

In a world where corrupt deception abounds, it is refreshing to have such a prominent company set a great example of just the opposite. But, written words are only a guide to follow; **it is your leadership, your example, your culture that will determine your success.**

Now, fast forward 100 years later to Zappos, the billion dollar internet shoe company; they too, require their new hires to memorize their company's **10 Core Values**. They require everyone they hire, regardless of position, (from customer service reps, accountants, lawyers, to software developers) to go through *the same 4-week training program* in which they study company history, the importance of customer service, the long-term vision of the company, company philosophy, and corporate culture.

In fact, at the end of each week of training, Zappos offers anyone $2,000 to quit ... which is a standing offer until the end of the fourth week. They are looking for people who want careers not jobs. Less than 1% of the people take them up on the offer.

Two companies,
starting 100 years apart,
are living by the same values.

▶ Both companies believe the best way to build a brand is long-term.

▶ Both companies believe in fantastic customer service.

▶ Both companies believe in having passionate employees.

▶ Both companies believe that if you get the culture right, most everything else will fall in place.

While you are creating a culture of ownership, may I suggest you also make it a "Humble" culture. One of the biggest destructive forces today that causes countless large companies to fail is an ATTITUDE of ARROGANCE.

Bill Gates said, *"Success is a lousy teacher. It seduces smart people into thinking they can't lose."* Couple that statement with one from former Intel Chairman Andy Grove, who said, *"Only the paranoid survive. Paranoids believe someone or some force is out to get them,"* and now you should have a better perspective on how two enormously successful men remained successful in such competitive, turbulent times. I think it is extremely important to be confident but not arrogant. I find arrogant people to be resistant to evaluation and challenges, have a false sense of invincibility, and are especially close-minded to listening to what others might suggest.

The business landscape is littered with powerful companies who thought they were invincible only to find they were vulnerable to smaller, more nimble companies. Success teaches us that if we keep doing the same thing, the same way, we will keep being successful. That might work "until" your competition starts following everything you do to the letter, then it is time for you to raise the bar. You shouldn't fear your competition, but you should certainly respect them.

Realize your only true security in life is...

- **your ability to perform better than your competition**
- **your desire to improve, learn and study**
- **your persistence to constantly keep moving forward**
- **your consistency in delivering more than is expected**
- **your focusing on the most important matters**

Over-confidence (arrogance) destroys even the best of the best. So, explore failures to understand what happened, acknowledge weaknesses, seek advice from others, welcome suggestions, and stay humble. Understand, if you keep doing what you've always done … you will be gone. What are you doing this year to **RAISE YOUR LINE?**

LINE RAISER:
Create a culture of humble respect for your success
and be forever mindful that each day
you must prove yourself again.

CHAPTER 17
What is the Worst Thing That Can Happen?

I have heard it said over and over again that what holds people back from succeeding is the **FEAR OF FAILURE**. I think there is more to it than that. I think the phrase "FEAR OF FAILURE" is directly connected to FEAR of shame, FEAR of ridicule, FEAR of embarrassment, or the FEAR of humiliation. The sad thing about those fears is they are all self-imposed. We are the ones who give those fears value; the way to stop that concern is … ***Don't Give Your Consent.***

I personally understand all too well, that failing will stimulate feelings of disappointment, anger, and frustration. But that's okay. I have also found that those emotions, when channeled correctly, can be catalysts for overcoming the failed attempt. ***Meaningful Success*** comes from those who are willing to risk failure, willing to take risks, willing to stretch the boundaries, and willing to try something new.

Thomas Edison once said, **"I failed on my way to SUCCESS."** The key to handling a failure is to first and foremost, not call it a failure … ***it was an unsuccessful attempt at trying to accomplish something.*** There are countless reasons for failure; there were things that happened you didn't foresee, the design or process was flawed, you over-estimated your capabilities, you under-estimated your competition … etc., etc., etc.

What you should take away from any failed attempt is the ***knowledge of why*** you were unsuccessful. **NOW YOU KNOW why you failed is the essence, the key, the heart and soul of future success. NOW YOU KNOW** you should have zigged instead of zagged. **NOW YOU KNOW** you should have turned left instead of right. **The GREAT NEWS is … NOW YOU KNOW.** But, if you start worrying about what others will think because you didn't succeed the first time, you are wasting valuable energy that can be used to succeed the next time.

One of the main components in the **"Art of Making Decisions"** is ***can you live with the consequences*** if the decision you make ***goes wrong, doesn't work, fails, bombs, flops, is a loser, a fiasco, or a dud?*** If you can't live with the bad consequence(s) then you better look for an alternative solution. Some people may say, *"Well, I didn't see that consequence coming"* or *"I never thought of that possibility" ...* that is why, with critical decisions, you may want to solicit other peoples' opinions.

LINE RAISER:

When making a critical decision,
solicit other peoples' opinions,
and then decide if you can
live with the consequences if it fails.

If you can live with the consequences then
GO FOR IT!

There are lots of clever acronyms for F.E.A.R.

False Experiences Appearing Real
False Emotions Appearing Real
Future Events Already Ruined
Frantic Effort to Avoid Reality

or the one a lot of people seem to choose ...

Forget Everything And <u>Run</u>!

Don't let anyone tell you FEAR isn't real. It is very real ... but you can handle it. I am not addressing life or death situations here ... this is about the FEAR that is holding you back from:

- *moving forward in your life*
- *advancing your career*
- *decision making in a management/leadership position*
- *handling things-issues-situations life is constantly throwing at you*

The great hockey player Wayne Gretzky said, *"You'll always miss 100% of the shots you don't take."* The world renowned artist, Vincent van Gogh said, *"What would life be if we had no courage to attempt anything?"* The great ones don't worry about what other people will think … they **JUST DO IT**. (Sound familiar?) The other day I came across this statement from an unknown author that I think sums it up best of all …

FEAR has two meanings:

Forget Everything and Run
or
Face Everything and Rise

The Choice Is Yours!

I think having a **"Higher Line Mentality"** makes decisions easier. I don't care how hard the decision is, just simply ask yourself, *will my decision make my line (now or eventually) go up.* That one question takes everything out of the equation; fear, uncertainty, consequences are gone, and the decision you need to make becomes crystal clear.

CHAPTER 18
If You Want to Succeed
Then Start Focusing

The great companies (and leaders) today are staying calm, keeping a clear head, and then focusing their efforts on profitability, increasing cash flow and making their customers their number one concern. Discipline becomes the rule, and simplifying what they do best, the goal. Many companies lose sight of their core business. They get busy re-organizing or re-restructuring when they should be busy at under-promising and over-delivering in everything they do. Never confuse activity with accomplishment. A gerbil on a running wheel is extremely active, but is going nowhere.

Align your entire company or organization around a single priority. Please don't get caught up in those fancy, smart sounding business phrases of identifying your value-chain, brand development, image make-over, contrast methodology, or reorganization criteria, just to name a few. Get down to the simple questions of …

What is it that we do best?
What made us successful?

Everyone in your company needs to know what it is that you are striving to deliver to the end customer. It might be saying, *"We will be making the very best sandwich, with the freshest ingredients, in the shortest amount of time, following the best sanitary policies in our industry."* Or *"We will deliver your freight on time, every time, with no damage."*

LINE RAISER:
If you don't know where to focus,
then start by identifying all customer complaints
and look for the most common cause of those complaints.

Years ago I wrote ...

The day you forget you are in business
for the customer,
is the day you start going out of business.

Focus, direct, fixate ... preoccupy your company obsessively on your defined target and make sure EVERYONE knows what it is and how they are to be held accountable. By the way, the same holds true for personal improvement. Focus your efforts on a single priority and see it through. You will be amazed how many other things you do will also improve.

Fix What Needs Fixing

I see a lot of valuable time being wasted in companies with people trying to improve something that is already working great. It is important to always be looking for ways to improve, but it is more important to be working on things that need improving. I live, work, and operate by what I like to refer to as **The Stapler Principle.** This principle has helped me immeasurably in being more efficient, which can also equate into being more profitable.

THE STAPLER PRINCIPLE

Concentrate your resources on critical areas
that need improving before ever trying
to improve on things that work just fine.

Staplers are simple to use, accomplish their task effortlessly,
do what is needed, cost little to use, and seldom if ever fail.
They don't slow production, upset customers, affect morale,
destroy profits, or frustrate employees;
when correctly used they work just fine.

So, leave the stapler alone and go work on things
that need improving.

A lot of companies seem to complicate the process of improvement. The big question of ... where do you start ... seems to be the big problem. With so many issues to address, they flounder in the process. Rather than talk about how to get better, how to improve how to streamline, how to reduce costs, or how to deliver better service to your customer, I find it better to first identify the most important core competencies your company must possess to succeed.

A couple of years ago, a company that had been in business for over 80 years and was doing over $500 million in sales hired me to address ways they could improve their operations. My first step in the process was to have them send out an e-mail to all management personnel who would be attending my session and ask them to respond to me with their answer to the following question.

(in order of priority)
What are the 5 CORE COMPETENCIES
your company must have to be
a successful leader in your industry?

There were 11 responses (Core Competencies)
that received multiple agreement.

Innovation at all levels	*10 responses*
Great customer service	*6 responses*
Cultural accountability	*6 responses*
Excellent communication skills	*6 responses*
High performing and satisfied employees	*6 responses*
A vision based on the strengths of the company	*5 responses*
Great quality	*4 responses*
Leadership	*4 responses*
Flexibility to grow and adapt to a changing market	*3 responses*
Strategic Planning	*3 responses*
New product development	*2 responses*

When all the responses were tallied up **they had identified 116 different core competencies.** How in the world is a company supposed to improve when the management team is in such disagreement with the 5 Core Competencies necessary to succeed? I will get back to that question a little later on.

That same year I did a program for a multi-billion international company whose CEO knew they had a problem. He had called me and said:

"Rob, our company leadership is fragmented. I need to get them all on the same page, moving together collectively as a unit. I know there is far more power in a unit working together for a common goal than with all the fragmentation we are now experiencing. How can I identify to them just how fragmented we are that will really make a lasting impression ... thus causing them to see the need to change our ways?"

Having learned a few more things from the $500m company I had just worked with, I simplified the process of identifying the problem. Instead of asking for 5 Core Competencies, we asked for only one. We followed the same e-mail response tactic, but asked for only one response. The email read:

What should you concentrate on to be the most successful company in your industry?

All responses were sent to me, so there would be no possibility of the results getting out before the meeting. *The e-mail was sent to 97 senior managers who would be attending the meeting.* What would be your guess as to how many different responses I received? The number certainly surprised me. The following chart will show how many managers had agreement to one answer.

14 out of 97 responses	= 14.4%
10 out of 97 responses	= 10.3%
9 out of 97 responses	= 9.3%
8 out of 97 responses	= 8.2%
4 out of 97 responses	= 4.1%
2 out of 97 responses	= 2.1%
2 out of 97 responses	= 2.1%

But there were 48 more different responses to …

What should you concentrate on to be the most successful company in your industry?

A total of 55 Different #1's

Here are the responses they agreed to again:

Quality	14
Find and retain quality (talented) people	10
Exceptional Customer Focus – Service	9
Client satisfaction (happy)	8
Client relationships	4
Business development – grass root focus	2
Superlative technical performance in current jobs	2
Growth - Expand globally	2

Here are some other responses I received in the two programs:

Be consistent
The depth of the product range / variety
Think out of the box
We listen to customer wants & needs & deliver what they request
Use state-of-the-art technology
Customization
Ability to do what competitors will not
Sales support
Value engineering
Focus on doing very few things extremely well
Ability to create solutions for the customer
Investment in R&D to develop superior technology
Continuing education
Focus
Provide clear structure & organization for employees
Be flexible and open to change

Have integrity
Meet and assist others in meeting schedules
Keeping up with technology
Build and maintain quality relationships
Deliver what we promise
React quickly – showing people you care
Be Lean
Communicate effectively

Again, I'll ask you *... How in the world is a company going to improve when the management team is in such disagreement with the "1" Core Competency necessary to succeed?* We are not talking about what the general population of the company was thinking ... we're talking about what the senior management team was thinking. The CEO was right. His management was extremely fragmented, and when I showed everyone the results of our survey they were flabbergasted.

For the next two days they worked on deciding on their **#1 Core Competency** by clearly defining things like ...

Why do we exist?

What is our purpose?

What exactly is the business we are in?

How do we currently define success in our business?

Is there a better way to define our success?

I will be getting into more detail on this later on, but before we get too far removed from their list or responses, I want to point out one more critical error when it comes to successfully running a business, and that is the overuse of POWERFUL MEANINGLESS WORDS. Any salesperson can say things like ...

We have better quality

We give better service

We communicate better with our customers

We use only the best ingredients or materials

To make these phrases have power, they need to have facts, stories, and examples of what you mean. The same is true in management. Define what quality is. Define what great service is. Define what communication is. Define what great sales support is. I can go on and on with the list of words that need to be defined and so must you. If your desire is to beat your competition, to stand above them all, may I make the following suggestion:

LINE RAISER:
Make it *Standard Operating Procedure* that all powerful words are defined in detail so everyone in your organization completely understands what they mean.

AND

LINE RAISER:
Make it known that at any meeting your people know they can be stopped and asked to explain in detail the meaning behind any words they used.

The problem I have with many of the statements companies make about what it is they do is that they are not specific. Let's go back to Zappos, who went from zero to $1 billion in sales in 10 years, so I can give you a good example of how to be specific, detailed, and exact, when it comes to defining statements to employees and/or customers. Zappos makes a general statement …

WE FOCUS ON BUILDING ENGAGEMENT AND TRUST

They then go on to tell you what that statement means and how they intend to go about doing it, along with providing ten bullet points to help everyone fully understand how they intend to build TRUST and ENGAGEMENT.

Here are Zappos ten bullet points:

► Make customer service a priority for the whole company.

► Empower and trust your customer service reps.

► Don't measure call times.

► Don't force employees to upsell.

► View each call as an investment in building a customer service brand.

► Realize it is okay to fire customers who are insatiable or abusive.

► Make WOW a verb … part of your company's everyday vocabulary.

► Have entire company celebrate great service; tell stories of WOW.

► Give great service to everyone: customers, employees, and vendors.

► Find & hire people who are already passionate about customer service.

You can go even further with this by explaining what GREAT CUSTOMER SERVICE is. Examples, stories, accomplishments, testimonial letters are all great things to share with everyone in your company so they fully understand …

<u>What is it</u> that you do
and
<u>What is it</u> that you expect?

I really like simple terms that hit on critical core competencies. The next time you are in a meeting and someone gives a wonderful explanation about some new product, service or procedure … have everyone in the room listen for ***powerful meaningless words.*** Have everyone write them down as the person is making their presentation (no interruptions). Then, after the presentation, have everyone share their list of words. Immediately, everyone will recognize the points (words) that need to be better define. I call it the **WHAT IS IT** list.

Better customer service …   **WHAT IS IT?**
Faster delivery …   **WHAT IS IT?**
Better quality …   **WHAT IS IT?**

Once your people start understanding that a simple GENERIC STATEMENT will not be accepted, that being specific is the norm in everything you do, your organization will start becoming a highly efficient, better managed and more profitable operation.

LINE RAISER:
Make "WHAT IS IT" a part of your culture.
If something is said but then can't be defined,
then don't say it.

General, non-specific, undefined,
broad sweeping statements have no place in companies
that are highly successful.

CHAPTER 19
The Power of Asking Questions

I guess I am one of the fortunate ones that have **finally learned** the power of asking questions. It is amazing what can be accomplished or learned by just asking questions. You can become a better boss, manager, salesperson, friend, and spouse, by just asking questions. If you are the one doing all the talking, you are not giving yourself the opportunity to learn anything. If you want to learn something, why not ask a question and then be quiet and listen. Let their answers lead you to other questions.

I have found that in most cases, people love to talk. So, by asking questions and letting them answer, you are allowing them to do what they like, thus making them comfortable, resulting in their seeing you in a more favorable light. You can also steer the conversation in the direction you want it to go by merely asking the right questions, allowing them to tell you what you need to know.

It has been said that you can gain and hold someone's attention better with a question than a statement. As long as you ask questions in a manner that invites a response rather than putting them on the defensive, you will learn more about the person, situation, problem, condition, etc.

LINE RAISER:
If you want to be more successful, become more intelligent, and also be known as a great conversationalist, then start asking questions and listen intently.

Now, let's address ... **The Power of the Question: *Why?* ...** as it pertains to leadership. In many companies there are policies, procedures, manuals and rules that people don't have a clue why they are still doing them. There are so many things we do because ... *that's the way we have always done it.* We could learn a lot from a three-year-old when it comes to how to cull out unnecessary "stuff" in running a business. If you tell a three-year-old to do something, before you get the words out of your mouth, you will hear, **"Why?"**

Is the three-year-old asking that question to annoy you, or are they just trying to drive you crazy? In most cases, they don't know why, and it's our job to have the answer. Now, you can be the big, bad parent and just say, *"Because I said so,"* and make them follow your request blindly with no explanation … but, that technique doesn't work very effectively in the business world.

Your people need to have the answer to the *"Why"* questions. If you can't answer their challenge with good responses, if you are not really certain why that rule is in place or that procedure is being followed, then it's time to **get the answer** or **change what you are doing.** I have no idea who wrote the following case study *(I wish I did so I could give them credit)* but it serves as great examples of …

> ➤ the power of asking the question "Why?"
> ➤ the embarrassment of not having the answer
> ➤ how doing what you've always done may NOW be wrong

A delegation of artillery officers from NATO, were visiting their British allies. The foreign officers were treated to an incredible display of motorized artillery in action by the Brits. After all the explosions and recoiling of the guns had died down, a rather confused NATO officer approached one of the British officers and asked why one of the soldiers in each of the artillery teams stood at attention throughout the entire demonstration doing absolutely nothing.

"Why?" the British officer responded. *"That is team member number 6. He always stands at attention when the gun is in action."* The NATO officer then responded. *"If that is the case, why do you need six men on each of the gun teams? Wouldn't five be enough?"*

There was no immediate answer from the Brits. Later on, curiosity getting the best of them, they decided to find out. After hours and hours of research looking through volumes of military field manuals dating back decades, they finally came upon their answer. It seems the original job of gun team member 6 was to hold the horses' reins that had pulled the gun into position. Just how many years (decades) had passed since they no longer used horses to pull the large artillery guns around?

LINE RAISER:
Accept "Why" questions as opportunities to streamline operations, improve efficiencies, and increase profitability.

The problem with a lot of companies or managers is that they have created an environment where challenges by subordinates are not looked upon in a positive manner. In fact, they are considered as challenges to authority rather than an effort to try and make the company stronger. Some managers / bosses / CEOs have instilled such an environment of fear that they seldom, if ever, have anyone question their ideas, policies, procedures, or methods. If no one is disagreeing, adding their two cents, or giving any "real" input at your meetings, you are just wasting time and don't need to have a meeting. You probably won't be in business long either, if that's the way you run a company. That being the case, many subordinates sit on the side line, seldom, if ever sharing the opinions and certainly never challenging anything the boss suggests or implements. How can you get them to get involved without the fear of reprisal?

You need to give them the right TO CHALLENGE; assign them the task, and encourage their challenges by designating several of them at a meeting to be **The Contrarians.** Remember what I said in my introduction about how former President Kennedy would assign a person at each cabinet meeting **to take the opposite view** of what was being proposed, even if they agreed with it? Well, you need to do the same thing. You need to make it perfectly clear that their job is to try and shoot holes in the plan, find the weak points or destroy it altogether, if they can. You need to point out that the **Contrarian** is a person who takes an opposing view, especially one who rejects the majority opinion. If a plan, idea, or suggestion can't stand up to their tough questions, the plan sure won't stand up to the real world when you to implement it.

LINE RAISER:

**At every management meeting assign at least one person
to be *The Contrarian*;
even if they agree with your idea,
make them try to shoot holes in it, find fault,
or consider alternatives.**

Challenges keep companies healthy. May I also suggest that at each subsequent meeting you pick a different person to serve in the position of **Contrarian,** because people have a tendency to start disliking a person if they are always the one trying to shoot down ideas. Here are two examples of things that should have been challenged:

(Source: Great Government Goofs by Leland Gregory)

- One year, efficiency experts saved the Department of Defense $27 million. The only problem is the efficiency experts charged the DOD $150 million for their work.

- The El Paso, Texas, City Council approved $112,000 to retain a private security firm – to guard the city's police station.

Someone should have stood up in those meetings and said –

"Wait a minute..."
 "We have better things to do with our money."
 "This makes no sense!"
 "This is ridiculous."
 "You've got to be kidding."
 "Why?"

Always remember, when it's not their own money, attitudes are more accepting of stupid ideas. Just look at our own government; we have billions of tax dollars being spent on things we shouldn't be spending them on. But it's not money coming directly out of their pocket, so it is easy to spend.

Personally, I will take one Contrarian over a room full of "Yes" people; at least the Contrarian will force me to think. Never take offense from someone who is challenging your idea. Simple words like *"Why"* or *"What if"* can save a company if asked at the right time. Great leaders see challenges as an invitation for the group to test, justify, explain, and prove the idea. They welcome vigorous dialogue and debate. They see argument and disagreement as catalysts to better solutions.

A contrarian can also serve as a very useful tool when it comes to making final decisions, because if you had the answers to their challenges, then it sounds like you've got a pretty good idea. Understand it is critical that once a decision is made, ***everyone must do everything they can to make it work,*** because only through a unified commitment can success be obtained.

Look at the questions

Why? - Why Not? - Why Don't We Try?

as powerful, helpful, useful, beneficial, worthwhile, valuable and productive questions rather than confrontational. Nobel Laureate and physicist Richard Feynman said that it was no coincidence that

virtually all major discoveries in physics were made by those under the age of 25. When he was asked why he concluded, *"You don't know what you don't know."* I guess another way you could put it is, when you are unaware of something that supposedly can't be done, you go at it with a blind determination to see if it CAN be done.

Any time I do a strategic planning session for a company, I always ask them to make sure they have some of their younger talents in the room. If you want fresh, new ideas, I think it is only appropriate to have fresh, new, young employees in the room sharing their ideas. You won't hear statements from them like, *"That's the way we've always done it,"* because they've **never done it.** What you will hear are challenging statements like, **"Why,"** or *"Why not,"* or **"Why don't we try?"**

Don't misunderstand, I am not saying that the veterans in a company should be *"put out to pasture"* when it comes to coming up with ideas that will improve it. I think experience is an incredibly powerful resource. Intellectual capital is one of the most valuable assets of any company. However, what I am saying is, don't discount an idea from a young associate by saying … **"What could they know … they are too young to know anything … they haven't been here long enough to know how we do it at our company."**

In the mid 1800's the head of the Patent Office in Washington recommended that the Patent Office be closed, because everything that could have been invented had already been invented. That same Patent Office rejected the patent applied for by the Wright Brothers for their flying machine… stating they believed machines that were heavier than air could not fly. Someone forgot to tell the Wright Brothers. They just kept asking themselves … **"why, why not, why don't we try,"** and aren't we glad they did.

Our youth of today have **grown up in a world of speed, multitasking, constantly changing technology, where virtually anything is accessible through the Internet.** I don't care what they don't know … I want to hear what they want to change, I want to hear what they don't like, I want to hear what they think is stupid or is a waste of time.

LINE RAISER:
If you want to stay successful ...
then stay curious and keep asking
WHY, WHY NOT, WHY DON'T WE TRY?

I must now give you a caveat when it comes to asking questions. Sometimes, the answer you get will be the CORRECT answer ... but the WRONG answer. You see, sometimes we ask questions the wrong way or we ask the wrong questions ... but either way ... we can end up with CORRRECT but WRONG answers.

Great leaders and managers understand that information is key in making decisions and that questions, when asked properly, can be a powerful aid in soliciting this information. But, sometimes we think we are asking the right questions, only to get answers that are actually right, but of no help to us ... and definitely not what we were looking for. Let me give you a few examples of questions teachers asked their students that elicited correct answers, but not the responses the teachers were looking for.

Q: Give a brief explanation of the meaning of "hard water."
A: Ice

Q: Where was the American Declaration of Independence signed?
A: At the bottom

Q: Johnny, what is the chemical formula for water?
A: H I J K L M N O

The teacher's follow-up question to Johnny's response was ...

Q: Where did you get that chemical formula for water?
A: Yesterday you said the chemical formula for water was H to O.

Q: To change centimeters into meters you _____?
A: Take out centi

Q: Now that you have finished the final exam, how do you feel about taking this class?

A: If I had only one hour to live, I'd spend it in this class because it feels like an eternity.

NO ... these were not the answers the teachers were looking for. Question & Answer sessions with employees are an excellent way to solve problems in organizations, if the right questions are being asked. Below is a sampling of a few questions I think all managers/leaders should be asking, and have answered each year if they plan on being/remaining successful.

- What does it take to be successful in our business?
   (less than 100 words)
- In your opinion, where are we below average, failing, or need to improve?
- What is the most important thing we should concentrate on to be successful?
- What is it that we do best/worst?
- What is the dumbest thing we do around here?
- What things/procedures/policies do we have that you think are unnecessary?
- What suggestions do you have that could make us more profitable/efficient/better?
- If you could change one thing about our company to make us better, what would it be?
- If you were our competitor, how would you beat us?
   In other words ...where do you feel we are vulnerable?

To make this exercise in questioning more beneficial and constructive I would like to offer the following three suggestions.

1. Questions should be answered anonymously so there is no possibility of retribution against any responses someone makes.

2. Tell everyone that their responses need to be specific and explained; saying we need to improve quality or customer service is too vague.

3. They can attack anything about the company, but not a person.

A problem identified is a blessing because you can't fix what you don't know is wrong.

Asking the right questions will help you find those problems.

I was in my garage this weekend wondering where all the *"stuff"* came from. It is amazing how much *"stuff"* we can collect over the years that we really don't need to keep. The same is true in business. Companies collect *"stuff,"* add programs, create policies and procedures, layering new things on top of old things. Our government has done the same thing with our tax code; the total number of pages of our tax code, including all tax regulations and IRS rulings, is now over 70,000. The Department of Energy was created during the Carter administration **to lessen our dependence on foreign oil.**

Over three decades later the DOE has a budget of $24 billion per year with over 16,000 federal employees, 100,000 contract employees, and we are still dependent on foreign oil.

I think we all need to take a lesson from Wal-Mart when it comes to running a business, our government and our own personal lives. Years ago Wal-Mart introduced a contest, complete with awards and prizes of all sorts, trying to get everyone in the company to *identify the stupidest thing they do at Wal-Mart.* The contest was designed to help eliminate all unnecessary, wasteful and/or costly policies, procedures, rules, regulations, products, supplies, (etc.) which were not helping the overall profitability of the company. The idea was to focus on subtraction. Wal-Mart feels that...

Addition is the exercise of fools. Subtraction is the exercise of genius

I agree with Wal-Mart. In this time of economic turmoil and uncertainty, it will be the companies who focus on their core business, eliminating all ***"unnecessary stuff,"*** who will survive. I am currently doing the same thing in my business. It is good to always be looking ahead, creating new ideas, products, policies and procedures that will help your company prosper. Just don't forget to get rid of the unnecessary stuff along the way.

LINE RAISER:

Take a page out of Wal-Mart's success strategy
and have your own meeting on eliminating unnecessary stuff.

Your first question should be:
What's the stupidest thing we do around here?

Then shut-up and listen to what your
employees/associates have to say.

This one question can serve as the catalyst to spark
an amazing dialogue that will help your company improve.

Another benefit that will come from asking great questions is that the answers will sometimes force you to start seeing things from a different perspective; your success is dependent upon it. My next chapter will be addressing this much needed skill.

CHAPTER 20
Time for a Different Perspective

Sometimes it takes a different leader to make a team successful. Sometimes it takes a different environment to stimulate an idea. Sometimes you have to look at something from a totally different perspective, before it will make any sense to you. One of my favorite ways to stimulate different ideas is to take an existing procedure and tell everyone in the group that they can no longer do it that way. They have to come up with a totally different way to do it. I call it *"Looking for the Second Right Idea."*

For there to be continued success, you have to keep challenging the way you do things. I have a friend who can paint a picture upside down in front of thousands of people and then spin it right side up and everyone can then see what he painted. No one had a clue what it was until he spun it around. That is why I love to include different experience levels, talents, skills, backgrounds, education and gender in one group. **I feel the more diverse the group, the greater the potential to discover alternative ways to do something that may lead to improvement.**

By rearranging the letters of some words or phrases, you can form another word or phrase that redefines the original; this is called a *Cognate Anagram.* Here are some great examples:

PRESBYTERIAN	= BEST IN PRAYER
THE COUNTRYSIDE	= NO CITY DUST HERE
SEPARATION	= ONE IS APART
THE MONA LISA	= AH, NOT A SMILE
ASTRONOMER	= MOON STARER
DESPERATION	= A ROPE ENDS IT
THE EYES	= THEY SEE
GEORGE BUSH	= HE BUGS GORE
THE MORSE CODE	= HERE COME DOTS
DORMITORY	= DIRTY ROOM
SLOT MACHINES	= CASH LOST IN ME

ELECTION RESULTS	= LIES - LET'S RECOUNT
A SHOPLIFTER	= HAS TO PILFER
JENNIFER ANISTON	= NICE IN JEANS
SNOOZE ALARMS	= ALAS! NO MORE Z 'S
A DECIMAL POINT	= I'M A DOT IN PLACE
ELEVEN PLUS TWO	= TWELVE PLUS ONE
CLINT EASTWOOD	= OLD WEST ACTION
STATUE OF LIBERTY	= BUILT TO STAY FREE
LISTEN	= SILENT
ACHIEVEMENTS	= NICE – SAVE THEM
ELVIS	= LIVES

I never thought DORMITORY would spell DIRTY ROOM or LISTEN could spell out SILENT. I once saw a collection of old discarded tennis racquets made into picture frames. Most people would have seen trash, where someone else saw a creative way to display pictures. So, the next time you think there is only one way to do something, get your point across, or accomplish a certain task – think again. Success in life comes to those who keep asking *"why"* or *"why not."* If you limit your perspective, you limit your chance for success.

LINE RAISER:
Include different experience levels, talents, skills, backgrounds, education, and gender in one group.
The more diverse the group,
the greater the potential to discover alternative ways to do something ... that may lead to improvement.

NARROW IS THE MIND THAT SEES THINGS FROM ONLY ONE PERSPECTIVE

One perspective you should appreciate "knowing" is that of your customer, especially an unhappy or difficult customer. Years ago I read an article in *The Harvard Business Review* that stated: ***"1 out of 25 customers complain, the other 24 go somewhere else."*** Those are extremely scary numbers. It doesn't matter if you do or don't agree with their findings. What matters is how you, your associates, your organization perceives an unhappy customer. Are they perceived as a complainer, bellyacher, griper, villain, and/or jerk? If they are perceived that way, you are going to need to do a major paradigm shift in this costly perception.

You need to label your outspoken unhappy customers as *CUSTOMER SERVICE CONSULTANTS*. They are unhappy customers who haven't walked away, <u>YET</u>. They are actually giving you the opportunity to correct a situation. Their complaint can help to serve as a contribution to the future success of your organization.

It is time to start viewing these difficult customers as **allies**. They can help your organization prosper by identifying areas of discontent. Thank them for their feedback, and if possible, figure out ways you can reward them for their feedback. Celebrate in the fact that you have been given a second chance *(which seldom, if ever happens);* a chance to fix, adjust, tweak a problem you weren't aware of. **You can't fix what you don't know about.** Be grateful they came forward, rather than deciding to say nothing and just go somewhere else.

CHAPTER 21

Chalk Up a "6"

Andrew Carnegie hired Charles M. Schwab to run US Steel in 1921 and paid him $1 million per year. That was $3,000 per day, when people who made $50 per week, were considered well off and there was no income tax. He was not hired because he knew more about steel than anyone else. Carnegie hired him because **he was a genius at dealing with people.**

There was a book written about Mr. Schwab back in 1912 entitled *Succeeding with What You Have.* I would like to pull a short excerpt from the book that gives a great example of how Mr. Schwab was able to motivate his people to accomplish more without threats, condemnation, fear, criticism, intimidation, or pressure. I'll be paraphrasing what was written.

When asked for the secret of his success in the steel industry, Charles M. Schwab always talked about making the most with what you have, **USING PRAISE, NOT CRITICISM, GIVING LIBERAL BONUSES FOR WORK WELL DONE,** and as he stated;

"Appealing to the American spirit of conquest in my men, the spirit of doing things better than anyone has ever done them before."

He liked to tell this story about how he handled an unproductive steel mill: He said he had a mill manager who was finely educated, thoroughly capable and master of every detail of the business. **But he seemed unable to inspire his men to do their best.** Mr. Schwab asked him one day ...

"How is it that a man as able as you, cannot make this mill turn out what it should?"

The manager replied ...

*"I don't know. I have coaxed the men; I have pushed them,
I have sworn at them. I have done everything in my power.
Yet they will not produce."*

The night production supervisor and his team could never produce as much steel as the day production team, EVER, and the day team wasn't doing that well, either. It was a few minutes before the night production crew was to arrive, so Mr. Schwab asked the day supervisor how many batches of steel his team produced that day. The supervisor replied **"6."**

Mr. Schwab asked for some chalk and in the front entrance of the steel mill, where everyone had to walk past to enter the steel mill, he wrote a giant **"6"** and then walked away saying nothing.

When the night shift came in they all saw the giant *"6"* and asked about it. They were told that …

*"The big boss was in here today and asked how many
batches of steel had been produced on the day shift,
and then "HE" chalked down the big "6."*

The next morning when the day-shift showed up they saw that the **"6"** had been rubbed out and a big **"7"** was written instead. The night shift had beaten them *(something they had **NEVER** done before)* … and also had thrown down a challenge at the same time.

When the day-shift saw the **"7"** boy did things start happening. By the end of their shift the **"7"** was rubbed out and a **"10"** written in its place *(something they had **NEVER** done before).*

Thus, a fine competition was started, and it went on until this mill, formerly the poorest producer, was turning out more than any other mill.

No one was ***coaxed, pushed, cursed, intimidated, yelled at, threatened, nor was fear used*** to get them to produce more. No threatening memos were issued or jobs ***on-the-line*** to get production up. A simple **"6"** was written where all could see … and things like *competition, resourcefulness, teamwork, rivalry, ingenuity, maximum effort, determination,* and *pride* kicked in. Mr. Schwab once said …

> *"I consider my ability to arouse enthusiasm among my people*
> *the greatest asset I possess,*
> *and the way to develop the best that is in a person is by*
> <u>*APPRECIATION*</u> *and* <u>*ENCOURAGEMENT.*</u>*"*

Almost 100 years later, Jim Collins, in his best-selling book ***Good to Great***, said the most frequent words used to describe the TOP 11 corporate leaders in America *(by the people who worked for them)* were … **Shy, Quiet, Modest, Humble, Gracious, Reserved, Understated,** and **Mild-mannered.** Some leaders "get it" … most don't. **One of the most important things a leader can do is "INSPIRE" the people around them to "WANT TO" do better.**

Fear is a Short Term Remedy
Inspiration is a Long Term Solution
Create The <u>WANT TO</u> not the <u>HAVE TO</u>

LINE RAISER:
Make <u>APPRECIATION</u> and <u>ENCOURAGEMENT</u>
the corner stone of your leadership style.
Try to incorporate competition, resourcefulness,
teamwork, rivalry, ingenuity, and a sense of pride
in everything you do.

I would like to address the last point of my suggestion, *incorporating a sense of pride,* a little further. There are a lot of great words in the English language that, for me, immediately get my attention when said. Words like guarantee, proven, freedom, trust, destiny, and love. When *"you guarantee"* something or say *"you trust"* someone ... that is a powerful statement; you are putting your reputation on the line.

Another word I really like is PROUD. It is defined as: satisfaction over something regarded as highly honorable or creditable to oneself ... stately or distinguished, bold or fearless ... to honor or distinguish a person or organization. It conjures up statements like:

Go out there and make us proud.
You really did yourself proud.
That was a proud moment for us.

When you make people PROUD of what you did,
then YOU DID GOOD!

One of my clients, Forward Air, asked me to design a program around their corporate theme they implemented, which has been so successful that they carried it over into next year. Their theme was based on the acronym P.R.O.U.D., which, for them, stands for:

Performance – Results – Ownership – Unity – Difference

I asked them if I could share a little of their corporate philosophy with you because I personally think it is a fantastic word to base a corporate culture around. They said, *"Go right ahead; share it with anyone."* Their objective (I am paraphrasing) was stated:

This year is all about showing pride in yourself, your job, your team, and your company through positive actions and striving to excel in all you do – to THINK, FEEL, and BE PROUD. Are you PROUD of the job you've done? Are you PROUD to be here? Did the experience make you PROUD? Does your team make you PROUD? They went on to state how to achieve PROUD.

PERFORMANCE:
Choose paths that generate positive outcomes –
avoid paths of least resistance.

RESULTS:
Reach beyond ordinary results – refuse limitations.

OWNERSHIP:
Own every opportunity; seize the smallest of opportunities –
make them extraordinary.

UNITY:
Understand the BIG picture; genuinely support united goals
and group success.

DIFFERENCE:
Dedicate to difference. Deny status quo, aim high and engage.

They had banners, t-shirts, mega-phones, stickers, and giant foam fingers imprinted with PROUD everywhere. The company also gives out monthly, quarterly, and annual PROUD awards. They want their people to…

THINK PROUD – it's all about the attitude.
FEEL PROUD – and show it in each task.
BE PROUD – by owning your job and stamp your name all over it.

Regardless if it is a corporate theme or just on a personal basis,
I think it is critical to …

LINE RAISER:
Always deliver your best – Accept nothing less.
When you put PRIDE in your work,
you will always be PROUD of the results.

CHAPTER 22
Put Down the Glass

Before I end my section on leadership, I think it is imperative to discuss one more aspect on the subject that I feel gets overlooked far too often; pushing yourself and your people too far. Years ago a speaker gave a great example on stress management *(the author of the example is unknown)*. He held up a glass of water and then told the audience…

"Let's estimate that the weight of this glass of water is one pound?
The actual weight of the glass of water isn't that important.
What is important in this example is how long you can hold it.
Holding it for a minute is not a problem.
Holding it for an hour – now that could cause your arm to ache.
But, trying to hold it for a day, would be nearly impossible
and damaging to your arm, wrist and hand.
In holding a glass of water for a minute, hour or day …
the weight of the glass will never change,
but as time passes,
the longer you hold it,
the heavier it will become."

He then went on to explain that the example is very applicable to stress management. Whether you want to call stress … burdens, responsibilities, or commitments from your job or family … without setting them aside and taking a break, at some point they will become too heavy to carry.

The longer you carry stress without a break, the less effective you will be in everything you do. Your body needs time to recharge, and your mind and mental attitude need some time to decompress so you will feel refreshed. When you are refreshed you are able to carry heavy burdens and take care of lots of responsibilities and commitments, **so the critical factor in all of this is … learning how to stay refreshed.**

The simple solution to staying refreshed and vibrant is to learn how to *put down the glass*. When you leave the office don't carry your work home with you … *put down the glass*. When you go on vacation don't check e-mails or voicemails … have them forwarded to an associate who can handle them … *put down the glass*. If you want to be more effective in everything you do, you have got to *put down the glass;* relax, exercise, or spend some "fun" time with your family.

LINE RAISER:

If you are in management
and you want your people to be
more effective, productive, and innovative,
make sure you are giving them time to

PUT DOWN THEIR GLASS;

the glass will surely end up broken if you don't.

Note: This suggestion applies to everyone.
Some organizations think management (leaders)
should be on call 24/7 … 365 days per year.
Being in management
does not make you immune to BURNOUT.

Everyone Needs to Put Down Their Glass.

SECTION 3

Raising Your Line
As a Company

CHAPTER 23
We Are All Responsible for Sales

One of the biggest mistakes any company makes is not educating everyone in their organization that they are "ALL" involved in SALES. **Nothing happens without sales being made ... nothing!** Great customer service helps bring customers back ... but so many people in companies feel that because they may not have any direct contact with a customer, client, patron, consumer, (*whatever it is you want to call them*) then they have nothing to do with sales.

Nothing could be further from the truth. The end result for any organization must be a happy customer and it takes all departments, all personnel doing their job properly, to make that happen. So, since we are all involved in sales, I thought it appropriate to set the tone of this section and start off with how important salespeople are to every organization.

So many times I am brought into organizations to talk about sales and I see/feel that some of their salespeople really don't want to be called, or considered salespeople. Management even goes out of their way to figure out a different title for them such as ...

Account Executive, Account Manager, Advisor, Business Counselor, Business Development Manager, Consultant, Customer Representative, Customer Specialist, Marketing Engineer, Marketing Manager, Relationship Manager, Solutions Analyst, Technical Sales Advisor, etc., etc.

It is as if they aren't proud of being in sales or being considered a salesperson. For you folks out there who aren't proud of being in sales ... or ... for those of you who might look at salespeople in a different light as compared to how you would value some other business executive ... I want to share a little piece I found years ago that sums up the true value salespeople bring to any company. The author is unknown, but whoever wrote it ... got it right! I've taken the liberty of tweaking the original article to make it a little more current.

I am proud to be a salesperson because more than any other person I, and millions of others like me, built America. The people who build a better mousetrap - or better anything - would starve to death if they waited for customers to beat a pathway to their door. **Regardless of how good, or how needed the product or service might be, it has to be sold.** Eli Whitney was laughed at when he showed his cotton gin. Edison had to install his electric light free of charge in an office building before anyone would even look at it. The first sewing machine was smashed to pieces by a Boston mob. People scoffed at the idea of railroads. They thought that even traveling thirty miles an hour would stop the circulation of the blood! Morse had to plead before ten Congresses before they would even look at his telegraph.

The public didn't go around demanding these things; they had to be sold! **They needed thousands of salespeople, trailblazers, pioneers, people who could persuade with the same effectiveness as the inventor could invent.** Salespeople took these inventions, sold the public on what these products could do, taught customers how to use them, and then taught business people how to make a profit from them. As a salesperson I've done more to make America what it is today than any other person you know. I was as vital in your great-great-grandparents' day as I am in yours, and I'll be just as vital in your great-great-grandchildren's day. I have educated more people; created more jobs; taken the drudgery from the laborer's work; given more profits to business people; and have given more people a fuller and richer life than anyone in history.

I've dragged prices down, pushed quality up, and made it possible for you to enjoy the comforts and luxuries of automobiles, radios, electric refrigerators, televisions, and air-conditioned homes and buildings. I've made it possible for inventors to invent, for factories to hum, and for ships to sail the seven seas. How much money you find in your pay envelope next week and the future success of products yet to be invented will depend on me. **Without me the wheels of industry would come to a grinding halt.** I AM A SALESPERSON, and both proud and grateful that as such I serve my family, my fellow man, and my country.

I hope this chapter makes you all look at salespeople in a more positive, appreciative way, because they deserve it. Remember what I said at the start of this chapter - **Nothing happens without sales being made ... ABSOLUTLEY nothing!**

To help prove my point about everyone being involved in sales, I'd like to share story about an exceptional company I worked with. Several years ago I had the opportunity to present two programs to one of the leading property casualty insurance companies in the country, Cincinnati Insurance. They have been in business since 1950 and now have over 2,900 associates working at corporate and over 1,000 working in the field as Field Claims Representatives; from their humble beginnings they have grown to a multi-billion dollar corporation.

After I had presented my programs, one of their senior executives asked me what I found to be the most interesting fact I had discovered about their company while I was doing my research to prepare for the engagements. I replied,

> *"That's easy ... you don't advertise.*
> *You're doing several billion in sales with no advertising."*

He responded,

> *"Our claims department is our advertising;*
> *that is where we shine.*
> *Our Field Claims Representatives*
> *are our Promise Keepers.*
> *An insurance policy is only as good as*
> *how well the Promise is backed-up.*
> *We believe that if you deliver exceptional service,*
> *people will hear about you."*

The most powerful and trusted advertising in the world **is** "Word of Mouth." It is the most powerful "positive" advertising if you are doing a good job and the most powerful "Negative" advertising if you are doing a bad job. That being the case, everyone in a company has some direct or indirect involvement in selling your goods or services.

Note: To keep up with competition, Cincinnati Insurance now runs an occasional advertisement; things change, competition increases, and great companies adjust.

You may have, a big company, an incredibly sophisticated website, hundreds of locations, a huge advertising budget, thousands of employees, a phenomenal IT department, and an impressive Board of Directors … but do you have just one person I can talk to on the phone, one person who can help me, one person who speaks my language fluently, one person who has some authority, one person who listens well, one person who follows up after my call?

Or do you have a system that … puts me on hold for an extended length of time, has 2, 3, 4 verbal menus to navigate, never has a human answer the phone, makes it difficult to call your company, takes days or weeks to respond, frustrates, disappoints, exasperates customers?

A while back I called Prudential Life Insurance to get some information on a few annuities I have with them. Within minutes I was speaking to a highly competent person, who seemed happy to help me, **who spoke my language fluently** *(I didn't have to try and figure out what they were saying to me),* who listened attentively, never interrupted me, and answered *all* my questions. They even made a suggestion that would help me out later and instantly sent the form I needed. Let's just say I was extremely impressed and they didn't ask me to take a survey after the call. Just one person made it all happen.

Another time I called my bank on an issue with one of my accounts. The person I wanted to talk to was out, so I was sent to another person who was on the phone. I had to leave a message on their voice mail system. Two hours passed with no response. I called again and still couldn't get anyone to help. I called a third time hoping I would reach them but they were still busy. I called another location and did reach someone who figured out what had happened to my account, but told me it had to be resolved at the branch where I had my accounts. I called a fourth time and asked for the branch manager, but they were busy too, so I left another message. I even went on-line on their very fancy website and left a very unflattering email. I told them I had started yesterday at 9:30 am trying to get an answer to my question, and twenty-eight hours later I have heard nothing. All I wanted was to speak to just one person who could help me. By the way, within 100 yards of their location are five other banks.

I have already made this point, but I think it is such an important one that I'm going to make it again; **if you want to find out how good your company is, call it with a problem.** See how long it takes to get it resolved, how many messages you have to leave, how many menus you have to navigate to get to the one person who can help. Have your senior management team do it every week. Get them living the real experiences your customers are living and let your Customer Service People know that they are being called all the time by people who are checking up on them. In today's poor economy, with cut-throat competition, you can't afford to push your customers away because they can't reach just one person who can help them.

Prudential gets it ... does your company GET IT?

LINE RAISER:

**If you want to be successful,
get everyone in your organization understanding
how their job affects the sales process.**

**Identify their roles, show the importance,
and explain the costs of failure.**

CHAPTER 24
What are You Promising Them?

When I was getting towards the end of finishing writing this book, one of the publishing houses I was considering working with asked that we set-up at face-to-face meeting to discuss it in detail. In the meeting I encountered an excellent question from their senior editor. We were discussing the book title, chapter arrangement, and final content when she asked,

"Rob, what are you promising the reader
your book will do for them?"

She went on to say that,

"Every page you write should deliver on that promise,
therefore, everything should be predicated around
what you are promising the reader."

I believe her question is not only smart, powerful, and insightful for writing a business book, but is also extremely applicable to trying to figure out how to be successful in business.

SUGGESTION:

Ask and *Answer* this question yourself about your company:
"What are you promising the customer
you will do for them?"

Some corporate leaders might tell you they have "their promise" written in their vision, mission, or values statement. Some companies may even carry it as far as trying to convey "their promise" in their advertising slogan. Here are some great examples of companies advertising "their promise:"

❖ Way back in 1952 KFC said their chicken was *"Finger lickin' good!"* and they followed that slogan with *"We do chicken right."* But, just having great tasting chicken will not keep the customer coming back if the service is slow, attitudes are poor, and the place looks dirty.

❖ United Airlines wants us to believe that when you fly with them all their people are going to be friendly because their slogan is: *"Fly the friendly skies of United."* Trust me when I tell you, having flown millions of miles over the last 25 years to speaking engagements, there are times that the word "friendly" never enters my mind when I fly United or numerous other airline carriers for that matter.

❖ Disneyland says they are *"The happiest place on earth."* Not only do I agree with that, I would add they are also an amazingly clean amusement park.

❖ In 1962 Avis said, *"We try harder,"* trying to convince potential customers that they are working harder than Hertz, so they can take over for Hertz as the #1 car rental company. I get what they are trying to do, but they also just drew attention to the fact they aren't #1 and lots of folks like to deal with the best. *(and they still aren't #1)*

❖ FedEx gets it: They have a slogan … *"When it absolutely, positively has to be there overnight,"* and having worked for them numerous times, I can truly attest they are doing everything humanly possible to make sure that they live-up to that slogan.

A *"Generation Y"* (Millennial) might put it a different way:

"What's your deal, man?"

Well, that's my question to you: **What is your deal? What is your promise?** More importantly, does everyone in your company know that? You should consider what it is you really do and how you want to deliver that product or service. What is it that you value most? How do you want to be perceived by your customers?

This "Promise" is the driving force behind all goals and the glue that unites your employees, keeping them focused on the performance they need to deliver every time.

- ➢ *My flight attendant better be friendly*
- ➢ *My truck better be built like a ROCK*
- ➢ *My coffee better be good to the last drop*
- ➢ *My sub sandwich better be fresh*
- ➢ *You better let me have it my way*
- ➢ *My soup better be M'm M'm good*
- ➢ *That candy better melt in my mouth and not in my hand*
- ➢ *That battery better keep going and going and going*
- ➢ *My watch better take a licking and keep on ticking*

Are you thinking, *they said it on TV... they wrote it in ads... I heard it on the radio... THEY PROMISED!* Remember what the senior editor told me about book, *"Every page needs to deliver on that promise."* In business, success comes to those companies who get their people to understand what they are PROMISING their customers and then deliver on that promise, so, *"What's your deal?" ... "What's your promise?"*

Success Doesn't Come From Good Intentions
Success Comes From Keeping Promises

LINE RAISER:
Identify what you are promising to your customers
and make sure everyone in your organization understands
that "Promise" and how you intend to deliver upon it.

Now that you have identified what you are promising your customers, start making it part of your ***Corporate Culture*** that you only have **"One Chance"** to deliver on that promise. Today, in most cases, with all the competition that exists in the marketplace, one chance is probably the only chance customers will ever give you.

Companies spend lots of money on advertising for their customers, training employees how to politely deal with customers, trying to deliver the best product or service possible, and then somewhere along the process of dealing with the customer, "SOMEONE" drops the ball. Someone has a bad day, or gets frustrated, or is too busy, or thinks that's not their job, or they treat the customer rudely, impolitely, disrespectfully, or just have a PERSNICKETY attitude and you LOSE a customer.

But hey, it was only one customer; no big deal. REALLY? In today's social media world, it is never just one customer. Customers now have the opportunity to spread the word with just one click on a computer or cellphone and, BAM ... the story of bad, terrible, awful service is out. *(Bad news travels fast)*   Henry Ford once said,

> ***"It is not the employer who pays the wages.***
> ***Employers only handle the money.***
> ***It is the customer who pays the wages."***

That statement needs to be prevalent throughout your organization; every employee needs to understand where their paycheck comes from. **The moment an employee has any form of interaction with a customer, a BELL needs to go off in their head, reminding them of the critical importance of what is about to take place.** The customer has made a decision to do business with you at this moment ... **how YOU do, will determine if the customer will do business with your firm again.**

It has been said that ***opportunity never knocks twice at any person's door.*** So, you must always take advantage of your **first opportunity** and deliver. It is not just in customer service that ***Persnickety, Rude, Impolite, or Disrespectful,*** attitudes can hurt you. Many a career/relationship has been damaged, delayed, altered, or destroyed by a bad attitude.

LINE RAISER:

Make it a theme in your company to approach every
opportunity, task, job, interaction, or request
from a ONE CHANCE perspective.

You have ONE CHANCE to do it right
ONE CHANCE to impress
ONE CHANCE to win them over
ONE CHANCE to deliver.

**A good ending starts with a good beginning
so make your first impression count.
You have only ONE CHANCE to do that.**

You *Raise Your Line* in Business

by adhering to a

One Chance Mentality.

CHAPTER 25
Adequacy is Unacceptable

Now that you have identified what we are **"Promising the Customer,"** and that you should approach that promise as if you have only **"One Chance"** to deliver … let's now consider just how good you should be at following through on that promise. I recently did a program for The Dependable Companies who have been in business for 65 years. In researching the company to prepare for my program, I was really impressed with their *Value Statement*. It had such power and clarity incorporated into one short sentence. Here is their statement:

In the pursuit of excellence, adequacy is unacceptable.

After reading all the materials they had sent me, I asked their CEO, Ron Massman, to tell me what he thought was "THE" most important point, principle, statement, rule, mantra, they followed to be successful. He said,

"Rob, that's simple … adequacy is unacceptable."

There was no hesitation or need for reflection given to his answer. I asked, and in the *blink-of-an-eye*, I had my answer. Ron understands what is necessary to survive and thrive in business today. He believes in his corporate *Value Statement* … and he lives it. It guides him in all his business decisions.

The Internet, Facebook and Twitter (all Social Media) have changed the way companies must do business if they plan on surviving. People are going online and checking you out. They can go to "Angie's List" and see what is being said about you. Potential customers can simply type in their Goggle bar … **complaints about "your" company** and in one click, your chance of doing business could be crushed if the comments are lousy, bad, awful … or in some cases … *a terrible experience is described in such a detailed and colorfully descriptive manner, that you feel you just witnessed it yourself.*

People don't go online and write comments about adequate companies. They like to write about either **GREAT EXPERIENCES** or **BAD ONES**. Smart companies understand this trend and are doing everything they can to have client comments include words like ...

SUPERIOR, ASTONISHED, WOW, AWESOME, INCREDIBLE, AMAZING, SENSATIONAL, REMARKABLE, EXTRAORDINARY, and WONDERFUL.

I had two heat pump units installed in my house last week and the installers did an **incredible job**. They were on time, polite, professional, and respectful of our home and property, they didn't damage anything and cleaned up to make everything look just as it had before they arrived. Who gets fired up about heat pumps being installed? ME! They could have been late, rude, dirty, damaged my walls, trampled my shrubbery, not cleaned up all the debris, and taken a lot longer than they said was necessary. Cox Heating and Air Conditioning in Clearwater, Florida, understands great service.

If you plan on staying successful in business or want to advance your career, then understand that **adequacy is unacceptable.** To me, the word ADEQUATE is just another way of saying AVERAGE ... and average is something I have no need for. I don't want to hire average people or do business with average companies.

The CONSEQUENCE of just being ADEQUATE
is
DISAPPOINTMENT.

You *captivated* no one, you did nothing *exceptional, distinctive, excellent, unique,* or *outstanding,* and you certainly DID NOT *differentiate* yourself from your peers or competition. **Think about what would IMPRESS those you are working for and go for it.** A person/company who will do more than expected every time and do it with a smile on their face will find themselves in HIGH DEMAND.

> # LINE RAISER:
> Do more, be more, give more, and you will achieve more.
> There are no trophies, victories, or accolades
> given for adequate.
> I'll say it again:
> Think about what would <u>IMPRESS</u>
> those you are working for and go for it.

So, if you are in the pursuit of excellence, and you know that adequacy is unacceptable ... then why not shoot for PERFECTION?

Nadia Comăneci scored **the first perfect 10** in gymnastics for women in 1976; in fact, she scored seven of them in the 1976 Olympics. **Something that had never been achieved before by a female gymnast, she did seven times.** The scoreboard couldn't even show her score correctly because it had been manufactured so it could only display two numbers with a decimal place. When they showed her score they showed it as 1.0. *The scoreboard manufacturer was told no one would ever receive a perfect score (10.0) so don't build a three digit display.*

A perfect game is defined by Major League Baseball as a game in which a pitcher(s) pitches a victory that lasts a minimum of nine innings and no opposing player reaches base. The feat has only been achieved 22 times in the history of major league baseball.

Since the National Football League began in 1920, only one team has played a complete perfect season (both playoff and regular season): the 1972 Miami Dolphins, who won their fourteen regular season games and three postseason games, including Super Bowl VII, to finish the season 17–0–0. Apart from the 1972 Dolphins, three other NFL teams have completed undefeated and untied regular seasons: the 1934 Chicago Bears, the 1942 Chicago Bears, and the 2007 New England Patriots.

I think we should all strive for perfection. I don't believe any company, organization, association, team or person should accept *"that's good enough."* I read an article the other day stating that the airline industry loses 26 million bags per year; domestically they lose 2 million bags. Domestic airlines *"claim"* that 99% of the bags they handle eventually get to their customers … but if you are one of the 2 million who has a bag lost, you're not happy … and unhappy customers don't come back.

Ray Kroc founded the McDonald's Corporation in April of 1955, and I can personally attest that I have NEVER had a "BAD" french fry, hamburger, or Big Mac … EVER; not once in over 1,000 meals. The problem with so many companies is they have not defined what is considered perfect in the eyes of their customers … therefore, employees don't realize when they fall short. From cleanliness, to attitude, to speed, and accuracy (to name a few) … **what should be considered as perfect in your line of work?** Define it, post it where everyone can see it, and make sure you celebrate and reward those who achieve it. In sports, we can easily see when perfection has been obtained. The same needs to be done within your organization.

LINE RAISER:

Define perfection.
Make everyone aware of what it is.

You will be amazed how productivity will increase,
how customer satisfaction will surge and profits will soar
when the bar for perfection has been defined
and recognition given when achieved.

To RAISE YOUR LINE
as a company or an employee, always strive for perfection.
Remember … Adequacy is Unacceptable.

I personally think a great way to guarantee your success in life and business is to set the bar at the **ASTONISH** level. There are a few companies out there in the world today who have learned to raise the bar past WELL DONE, past REALLY WELL DONE, and even past the highly impressive accolades of GREAT or WOW. These few companies have taken it upon themselves to totally differentiate their organization from their competition by going above and beyond what a typical customer might expect as excellent service.

These few companies have decided, when at all possible, to ASTONISH their customers. They have looked at all the "customer service" statistics and data and taken it upon themselves to keep getting better and better, and do things that will impress and amaze their customers. Why should any company go to such lengths to do such a thing? Well, one thing you might want to consider is that statistics show loyal customers are, on average, worth 10 times as much as their first purchase. They have also found that this year only 37% of the companies in the U.S. earned a "good experience" index rating, and only 8% earned a "superior" rating.

Is it possible to get better every year? I think so. Let me give you a surprising example of getting better. Look at the winning times in the 100 meters race for the last four Olympics:

2000 Olympics in Sydney
the winning time was 9.87 seconds

2004 Olympics in Athens
the winning time was 9.85 seconds

2008 Olympics in Beijing
the winning time was 9.69 seconds

2012 Olympics in London
the winning time was 9.63 seconds.

That is four Olympics in a row where these incredible "world-class" athletes found a way to improve upon the winning time.

A couple of weekends ago I was catching up on my personal "Things to Do List" and was blown away (in a good way) by a company I had to deal with. My wife has an OtterBox Defender for her iPhone that was looking very worn. We went into a store to try and buy a new outside "Skin" and were told they didn't sell them ... no one did.

BUT, the young man said I could go to the OtterBox website and in just a couple of "EASY" steps, they would walk me through how you can get a brand new skin, totally free, if yours has worn out. Yeah right ... easy steps ... totally free ... that will be the day.

Well it was easy, it was free, and get this – I sent in my e-mail on Sunday afternoon and received a response from OtterBox the same day. On Monday morning, they shipped my replacement request. They weren't making a dime on my order. In fact, my service request was a cost to them, not revenue ... but in less than 18 hours they had shipped it. Who are these folks? Welcome to ASTONISHING.

We just replaced our iPhones with an updated version and guess what protective case we put on all three of them? OTTERBOX, without question. They stand behind their brand and their customer service is ASTONISHING. If you want to beat your competition and be assured you will always have repeat customers, start figuring out how you can ASTONISH your customers. There is always room to improve if you set your mind to it.

LINE RAISER:
Establish a corporate culture to astonish your customers.
By doing so, you will always be in demand.

Also, strive to do the same yourself. If you want to advance your career think of ways you can ASTONISH your peers, associates, and boss, and watch your career flourish! Doing more than expected every time is a great way to start.

Remember, I said it was important to define perfection and make it understandable to your organization; that can be done in many different ways, using countless descriptive terms for defining your level of service. I don't want to get caught up in the semantics of what to call great, incredible, amazing, perfect, astonishing customer service ... that is up to you. I just want you to do it and then make it totally understandable to everyone who works within your organization.

I just used ASTONISH as a descriptive term for great customer service. Norma Seymour, the Senior Vice President of Service Delivery for Cayman National Bank, in the Cayman Islands, has a different term that is just as powerful. Before I tell you her term, I first want to address her business title for the position she holds. I love how descriptive her title is ... *Service Delivery*.

Ms. Seymour takes her job and title very seriously, and does everything she can to help everyone in her organization deliver, as she puts it, "DELIGHTFUL" customer service. I have had the opportunity to work for Cayman National twice, and in my research preparing for my programs, I have witnessed first-hand, just how hard they work at delivering the best customer service in their industry.

They know that great, exceptional, amazing, DELIGHTFUL customer service starts and finishes with their people.

The financial services market is highly competitive and just as soon as a competitor comes up with a new product or service, everyone else will have it in short order. One out of five bank customers move their money every year because of poor customer service; not products, not location, not interest rates, just simply **poor customer service.** To lose 20% of your business because of the way you treat customers is appalling. In some industries, that number is even higher.

One Harvard Business Review study on customer service stated:

> ➤ **15% of customers left because of quality**
> ➤ **15% because of price**
> ➤ **20% because of lack of attention**
> ➤ **50% because "Contact" from personnel was poor**

Those numbers equate to 70% of the customers who left ... did so because of the human side of doing business. OUCH!

Last year, Ms. Seymour asked me to address Cayman National at a "Pep Rally" she was having for her staff and I was happy to oblige. I decided to weave my remarks around their goal of delivering DELIGHTFUL customer service. If you do a synonym check on the word DELIGHTFUL you will get words like *agreeable, alluring, cheery, congenial, engaging, enjoyable, gratifying, pleasing, pleasurable, refreshing,* and *satisfying.* Those are some pretty descriptive and admirable words to live up to in doing business with anyone. I challenged them at their "Pep Rally" with the following list of words. Relating them with their DE-LIGHTFUL goal … I told them to:

De- liver........... every time in everything you do
De- monstrate... great service along with a great attitude
De- termined.... to be the best at what you do
De- mand......... the very best of yourself
De- velop......... great habits
De- sire............ to be the best
De- feat............ the competition with all of the above

Norma is a big fan of Tina Turner (me, too) and uses the song *"You're The Best"* as her theme song to get everyone pumped up at all her meetings. Some of the lyrics in the song are incredibly powerful. *"You're simply the best, better than all the rest, better than anyone, anyone I've ever met."* Cayman National creates a culture that strives to be better than all the rest, and it shows in everything they do.

LINE RAISER:
Delight Your Customers In All That You Do
and Success Will Surely Follow You

CHAPTER 26
Words Customers Don't Want to Hear

Companies spend millions of dollars in advertising trying to attract a customer only to run them off by saying the wrong words. It seems that on a daily basis I will reach some company on the phone and hear the words, *"All agents are busy right now helping other customers. Please hold."* If I were their competitor I would see that as a huge opportunity to take business away from them.

How companies handle their
Personal-Point-of-Contact
with their clients or potential clients
will determine if they succeed or fail
in this highly competitive business environment.

In my opinion, customers don't want to hear, *"All agents are busy right now."* Customers don't want to go to your website and search for answers. Customers don't want you to send them a tutorial on how to do whatever they are calling to ask *you* about. Customers don't want to have to answer 10 questions to help better direct their call to the right department. We want to TALK to a human. We want to TALK to a nice, friendly, and pleasant human. We want to TALK to a highly knowledgeable human. We want to TALK to someone who can give us answers. We want to talk to someone who can help us.

LINE RAISER:
Sit down with your associates and talk about
all the phrases, statements, and/or words
customers hate to hear.
Post those words so everyone in your company
knows what "not" to say to a client.

Here are a few examples of statements customers don't want to hear:

➢ *"You will have to take that up with my supervisor."*
➢ *"There is no one in who can help you right now."*
➢ *"There is nothing I can do for you."*
➢ *"Please go to our website."*
➢ *"I don't know - I just work here."*
➢ *"That's not my job."*
➢ *"All lines are busy now ... please hold."*
➢ *"Please e-mail us your complaint."*
➢ *"I will have to transfer you to another department."*
➢ *"We are experiencing a high volume of calls ... please call back."*
➢ *"I know the policy is silly but I didn't set the policy - management did."*
➢ *"We take calls in the order received - you have 17 people ahead of you."*
➢ *"Our company policy doesn't allow us to do that - I don't know why."*

I recently quit doing business with a company who said it would take 72 hours to get me an answer to a problem *they* had caused. I soon learned that was their standard answer for any problems they caused. Their response caused me to look for another company to work with and within 24-hours I was up and running. I will never forget one of the statements said to me by the new company, Benchmark Email:

> *"Mr. Stevenson, don't you worry about a thing. I will personally walk you through every step and show you how to do it and even do it myself on my end if it gets confusing. Our job is to get you up and running and make things simple for you."*

Needless to say ... I was very impressed. She said ALL THE RIGHT WORDS and then delivered.

> # LINE RAISER:
> I have already made this suggestion once,
> but I feel it is so important I am going to make it again.
> If you want to find out how good your company is
> ## ...call it...
> and see how long it takes you to reach
> a pleasant person who can help you.

Many times the words your employees or your answering systems say will do nothing but drive business to your competitor.

> # LINE RAISER:
> Spend less money on advertising and more money
> on educating everyone on what
> *"to say"* and *"not to say"* to customers.
>
> Your advertising might be driving them to your company,
> but what is said next ... may be driving them away, forever.

Your top business strategy should be a
satisfied customer.

Saying your top business strategy is *"satisfying customers"* and then not insuring that message gets out to all your people and they live by that mantra has been the downfall of lots of organizations. One of my favorite examples of this would be the story called ...

The $180 Million Dollar Guitar

On March 31, 2008, mild-mannered Dave Carroll was flying with his band on United Airlines. After his plane landed, while waiting to deplane, a lady sitting across the aisle from Mr. Carroll cried out: *"My God, they're throwing guitars out there."* Mike Hiltz, the bass player in the band, immediately looked out the window and observed his prized instrument being hurled to the ground, without any regard by the United Airlines baggage handlers. Dave's personal $3,500 Taylor guitar had already been thrown out of the plane and was badly damaged.

Mr. Carroll immediately tried to communicate this to the flight attendant, who cut him off saying: *"Don't talk to me. Talk to the lead agent outside."* He found the person she pointed to and that lady was only an "acting" lead agent, according to her, who refused to talk to him and disappeared into the crowd saying *"I'm not the lead agent."*

He spoke to a third employee at the gate and told her the baggage handlers were throwing expensive instruments outside. She dismissed Mr. Carroll by saying, *"Hun, that's why we make you sign the waiver."* Dave told her he had signed no such waiver, and even if he had, that would be no excuse for what was happening outside. She told him to take it up with the ground crew in Omaha.

To make an incredibly long ordeal short ... Dave spent almost one year trying to get United to pay the $1,200 it cost him to fix his guitar, and was denied countless times. He even said he would take $1,200 in travel vouchers from United, but was denied again. He tried over and over and over to get anyone from United to help and NO ONE would take ownership of the problem and responsibility for making it right. As Dave put it, *"United's system is designed to frustrate affected customers into giving up their claims and United is very good at it."*

With no possibility of getting reimbursed anything for the damage United caused, he realized that maybe he was going at it the wrong way. He was a songwriter, so the traveling musician told United he would be writing three songs about United Airlines and his whole experience. He said he would then make videos for the songs and offer them as a free download on YouTube on his own website, inviting viewers to vote on their favorite United song. He told them his goal was to get one million hits in one year; **United didn't care.**

In July 2009, the first *United Breaks Guitar Song* became one of YouTube's greatest hits and caused an instant media frenzy across all major global networks. Four days after he released the song, United's stock dropped 10%, **a plunge that cost United $180 million**, which could have purchased 51,000 brand new Taylor guitars.

It was only after the song was released and attracted world-wide attention that United then offered to pay for the damages. Dave declined their too little, too late offer. Dave released three songs and videos in all and wrote a book about his experience – please go buy his book: *United Breaks Guitars: The Power of One Voice in the Age of Social Media.* Dave says the United Airlines ordeal turned into a blessing for him by helping to launch his career. By the way, the original YouTube video, when I last looked, had over 15 million views.

The next time your customer complains, you should consider it a blessing, because they are giving you the opportunity to fix the problem. Look at complaining customers as if they are consultants identifying weak points in the way you do business and treat each one like they could be the next Dave Carroll.

If you want to succeed in business and RAISE YOUR PROFIT LINE, get customers singing your praises!

CHAPTER 27
Never Eliminate a
Critical Reason for Your Success

A couple of years ago I bought my wife, Annie, a *Kindle Fire* as an upgrade to replace the *Kindle* she owns and loves to use. I thought I was being really smart by getting her a product that had so many additional features **(it was faster, it would surf the web, the viewing screen looked better, it had a back light and it was also in color)**; big "*brownie points*" for the smart husband. Little did I know or ever expect, that the engineers who developed the *Kindle Fire*, would ... eliminate ... a CRITICAL function.

For you non-*Kindle* folks out there, what was really cool about the original product is that you could buy a book right out of the Amazon store from just about anywhere; if you could get phone reception then you could use the Amazon "*Whispernet*" feature and boom ... you could buy a book. Those brilliant engineers took out that feature and replaced it with Wi-Fi.

Now, don't get me wrong, having Wi-Fi on the device is wonderful, as long as you can GET Wi-Fi. But, what if you are out of range? Can you order a book at the lake or beach where there might not be a good Wi-Fi connection ... NOPE. In fact, our house has a new Wi-Fi modem, but Annie can't even order a book if she walks out on the back porch. REALLY!

Annie could sit on the sofa in the den and buy a book on her OLD, out-of-date, first generation *Kindle* with a couple of clicks... but not on her new, fancy, more expensive *Kindle Fire*. Oh no, that simple, endearing, CRITICAL feature is now gone. Naturally, being a man, and thinking I have more technical intellect than my wife (a legend in my own mind), I knew my wife had to be wrong. I immediately reasoned that she just couldn't figure out how to find the *Whispernet;* she must have missed something because there was no way the *Kindle Fire* engineers would leave OFF something as important as that!

To make a really long story short ... BOY WAS I WRONG! After much research and reading in chat rooms and going to the Amazon help desk ... I found they had done just that. I was so frustrated, that *my great plan of getting a better product for my wife to surprise her had blown up in my face* ... that I sent off a scathing e-mail to Amazon. They sent back the following reply:

> I understand your concern regarding the Kindle Fire. Currently Kindle Fire allows you to wirelessly download full color versions of books, newspapers, magazines, and blogs only through a Wi-Fi connection.

> I understand that introducing the feature of Whispernet option will be an added comfort to the Kindle Fire users.

> We are constantly working to improve the features and services available for all our kindle users. Our goal is to help you get the most out of your Kindle experience. It is always important for us to hear how customers react to all aspects. I'll let the Kindle team know that you are interested in this feature. I know they'll want to hear about your experience.

> They're always looking for ways to improve our Kindle offerings and may be able to make this feature available.

> Thanks for your understanding and we look forward to see you soon. Thank you for your inquiry. Did I solve your problem?

The two lines I broke out from their note and put in bold slay me ...

(1) ***introducing the feature of Whispernet***
(2) **always looking to improve.**

There is no introducing or improving with that feature .... it was on the original ... you took it off. WHY?

My wife hates that you TOOK OFF THE BEST FEATURE of your product and *if **Momma ain't happy, nobody is happy.*** They also wrote, ***"Thanks for understanding."*** Well, we don't understand and NO, you didn't solve our problem. If you go to the on-line Amazon chat rooms, you will find we are not the only *Kindle*

Fire owners who really miss the feature! So, what can we learn from all of this ... or simply my suggestion to you;

> ## LINE RAISER:
> In your quest to make a better product
> or provide a superior service
> never lose touch with the reason(s)
> why people do business with you.
>
> The only perception of
> how you are performing
> is in the eyes of your customers.
>
> YOUR perception doesn't count ...
> only THEIRS.

If you want to insure
YOUR PROFIT LINE KEEPS RISING,
never eliminate a
CRITICAL REASON for SUCCESS.

Chapter 28
Anyone Can Have a Great Idea

Unfortunately, for some companies, for an idea to have any clout or gain any traction or acceptance it has to come from someone high-up in management. Let me set the record straight on ideas:

**There is no rule saying GREAT IDEAS
can "only" come from senior management.**

Most printer manufacturers such as Dell, Hewlett Packard, Canon, Lexmark, and Epson use what is referred to as the "razor and blade" business model. They would be happy just breaking even on manufacturing printers because they know the real money is in selling ink. This business model got its name from the manufacturers of double-edged safety razors that had just one blade; the real money was in selling you the "replacement" razor blades, not in selling the safety razor.

Now think about the cost of a printer and cost of the ink to make the printer work. *(Chanel No. 5 perfume costs approximately $38 per ounce, while the equivalent amount of printer ink can cost up to $75)* The ink is where the "real" profit lies for printer manufacturers.

The U.S. General Services Administration estimated a few years ago that their annual cost of ink for computer printers was $467 million. Could it be possible to save up to 30% of that expenditure ($136 million)? The answer is a resounding, "YES." Research has scientifically proven that by simply changing the printing "font" we use to Garamond …from Times New Roman, Century Gothic, or Comic Sans, we can reduce the amount of ink we use by up to 30%. If we applied this finding to state governments, an additional $234 million could be saved annually.

I guess the study was done by some brilliant scientist or university professor with the letters Ph.D. after their name. An idea like this would never come from a middle school student – but it did!

It all started as a science fair project, where fourteen year-old, Suvir Mirchandani, was trying to think of ways to cut waste and save money. His project was so impressive that his teacher had Suvir submit his finding to the Journal for Emerging Investigators, a publication founded by a group of Harvard grad students. Sarah Fankhauser, one of JEI's founders said, *"We were so impressed. We could really see the real-world application."* Gary Somerset, media and public relations manager at the Government Printing Office, described Suvir's study as truly *"remarkable."*

There are no boundaries on great ideas. There are no age limits on business brilliance. Michael Dell founded Dell computers in his college dorm room and now he is worth about $15 billion. Bill Gates had already grossed $2.5 million in sales when he was 23, and now he is one of the wealthiest men in the world. Mark Zuckerberg, 28, launched Facebook from his college dorm room and grew it into one of the world's most successful businesses; he is now worth billions.

When you are trying to figure out ways to make your company better, don't LIMIT your ideas by only looking at the ones from senior management. Many times, the people out there on the frontline have a much better perspective as to what is really going on and can be far more insightful with ideas, than those who are sitting behind a desk.

I suggest you use the concept from the popular TV show, **"The Voice."** The judges have their chairs facing away from the stage and cannot see the person who is singing. They don't know if they are old or young, attractive or plain looking … they can only choose if they like the VOICE; nothing else can influence their vote. The "voice" is what is important. The same is true in business. The "idea" is what is important.

LINE RAISER:
The next time you have a meeting
and want people to share their ideas,
have them submit their ideas anonymously,
with each idea identified by a specific number
assigned to each person.
(don't identify whose idea it was until the end of the meeting)

Jack Welch, the former CEO of General Electric once said, *"The hero is the one with ideas."* Don't let age, tenure, gender or personalities influence if an idea is good or bad. Some people will shoot down an idea because they don't like someone, they haven't been with the company long enough, or they are too young to know what they are talking about. Remember, good ideas have no boundaries.

If you limit the amount of ideas you consider – you limit your potential for success.

You essentially are restricting your ability to Raise Your Line Higher.

CHAPTER 29
Greatest Company Asset – Your People

For more than twenty years I have had the opportunity of working with some amazing companies. One of them who stood out to me is **The F.A. Bartlett Tree Expert Company.** This company was founded in 1907 by Francis Bartlett and now has over 100 offices worldwide, with over 1,500 employees, and revenues of over $210 million.

Several years ago they invited me to speak at an annual company meeting. The night before my program they had a big banquet for all management personnel and invited me to attend. They told me I would be able to gather some extra insight about their company from the people I would be sitting with; they said to feel free to ask all the questions I wanted. I requested they tell (warn) the people sitting at my table that I would be collecting some additional material to add to my speech the following morning; *I didn't want them to think I was weird because I was asking so many questions.*

To open up the conversation, the first question I decided to ask was an easy one … *How long everybody had been working for Bartlett Tree?* Their answers were astounding. The youngest tenured person at the table had been with the company for 30 years; little did I know, he was a rookie compared to everyone else. There was one gentleman at the table who had been with them for over 60 years. I later found out the person who had been employed the longest at Bartlett was Carl Lundborg, who had been employed and on payroll with the company for 72 years. He was followed by Jack Good who had worked for the company for 67 years. These two men didn't see it as a job; it was their vocation, their calling, something they loved to do. I found out later, they were just the tip of the iceberg when it came to long-standing employment at Bartlett Tree.

When I called their Vice President of Human Resources, Victor Fleck, to get additional information about why people work for "SO" long for Bartlett … I was allowed to take a look at the soul of what makes their company so successful; **their people.** Victor, or Vic, as he likes to be called, has been with Bartlett Trees for over four decades, the majority of that time he has been their VP of Human Resources; *with what I had come to learn about how long people work for Bartlett ... that didn't surprise me.*

Vic was delighted to share with me their philosophy on running a successful business. He first informed me that twenty-three employees had reached fifty or more years with the company. This privately held, third generation-run company, which has been in business for over 100 years, sees their employees as their most valuable asset. It's a family owned company and they treat their people like family.

Let's go back to their two longest employed employees, Carl Lundborg and Jack Good. Carl was still working for Bartlett when he was over 90 years old. Jack was 85 years old and still working there. They loved coming to the office, sharing stories, and helping out any way they could with the new people. Carl was known for his incredible way with dealing with upset customers. He was best described as a "Wiz" at customer relations. He loved going out to meet with anyone who felt they had not been serviced the way they thought they should have been; he relished the opportunity of turning a bad situation into a good one, and was still doing it for Bartlett at 90 years old. WOW!

Carl and Jack were a treasure trove of knowledge and were able to call upon this knowledge to help the organization in so many ways. Right up to the day they died, they worked with sales people in the field, recruiting college students to come to work for Bartlett, and also with the production guys in the field when they encountered difficulties and needed suggestions on the way a problem could be solved. This wasn't a job ... it was a passion.

Bartlett knows their people are what makes their company so special. They know if you treat your people special, fairly, and with respect, they will do the same with their customers. They believe you should give everyone a chance to improve, give them a feeling of security, and make them as comfortable as being with family ... because that's what they really are ... one big successful family. They have established a nurturing culture where their youthful, inexperienced people are taken under the wing of the more experienced ones and helped. It's not about having a job ... it's about having a fulfilling career, surrounded by people who care about you, your family, their industry, and their community.

The F.A. Bartlett Tree Expert Company provides scholarships at over 25 colleges and universities throughout the country trying to ensure the success of their industry and their way of doing business. They have to fight hard in a highly competitive industry that has a lot of competitors. They know the only way to win is by having the best working for them and keeping them at Bartlett.

When employees win awards the Chairman of Bartlett Tree, Robert Bartlett, the President, James Ingram, and Vice President of Human Resources, Vic Fleck take each winner and their significant other out to dinner. It is an up-close and personal time spent with the people who are going out of their way to help make Bartlett the leader in the marketplace. As Vic said, *"When our people go out of their way to make us look good, we go out of our way to make them feel good."*

Greg Daniels, *(their former President, who retired after 40 years with the company and remains active on their Board of Directors),* told me they work extremely hard at hiring, but even harder at keeping the right folks working for them. He said, *"It is disruptive and costly to bring on the wrong people, only to have to let them go later one. Their objective is to keep building on their knowledge base by maintaining a work environment that will not only enhance their company but their people as well."*

Bartlett understands the real expenses involved in hiring, training and then losing an employee. According to some industry experts in employee recruitment, it has been stated it takes over five months before an employee is really contributing to the profit margin of a company rather than being an expense on the bottom line. Bad employee turnover ratios can be very costly to any company and Bartlett does everything they can to insure the continued employment of the people they have working for them.

I have heard it said that "knowledge is power." I don't believe that to be right. **It's the proper use of knowledge that is power**. Bartlett believes that statement is a major component to their formula for success. The longer an employee works for them, the smarter and more experienced they become, and the more of a contribution they can make to the company.

Bartlett doesn't believe in fancy formulas for success. Their hidden ingredient, their secret formula for success lies in the right hiring, having the right training, and then making sure their employees are treated right. Is it working? Let's see … over 100 years in business, twenty-three employees who have been with the company for over 50 years and during the last recession, which was the toughest economy we have encountered since the great depression, they grew 10% … I'd say it is working.

Great companies come from building a strong foundation by finding, hiring and keeping the right people. In companies today, their *President, Senior Management,* and *Managers* can't be everywhere or do everything. As a company grows, it becomes a living, breathing, **mimicking** organization based on the principles portrayed by management.

LINE RAISER:

Establish a two-way mentoring program where the seasoned veterans help bring along the new folks *(young)* and share their experiences / knowledge and have the young folks share their expertise in current social media, software, apps and technology (etc.).

When you have the right principles in place, combined with the right people, and make sure your employees and associates follow those principles, good things happen and "All Lines" keep rising.

CHAPTER 30
What's Their Job?

According to the United States Small Business Administration, there are over 23 million small businesses in the United States, accounting for 54% of all sales and 55% of all jobs. The number of small business has increased 49% since 1980, and you might be surprised to know that big businesses in the U.S. have lost 4 million jobs since 1990, but small businesses have added 8 million jobs.

There are a lot of different criteria for being classified as a small business, so let's just simplify all of them and say we are talking about companies who have revenues between $1-$22 million. I have a pretty good knowledge of these type of companies because I, at one time or another, owned and operated five different companies. Now as a speaker and consultant, I work with them all the time. There are over 89,000 business associations in the U.S. which are made up of primarily small companies. Let's just say that "Entrepreneurship" is still alive and well in America, even with all the crippling government regulations; but that is a topic for another day.

One of the biggest problems I see with entrepreneurs is they are very good at their craft but lacking in some of the necessary business skills needed to properly run a business, or sometimes just too busy to deal with them; the latter is probably more the case. One place many of them drop the ball is in job descriptions. They hire people they desperately need only to throw them out on their own without a full and complete understanding of what is expected of them

What is their job description?
What is it they are supposed to do every day?
How will they be graded-rated-evaluated on doing their job right?

These are three great questions that all employees should be able to answer about their job/position/duties. The problem with most companies, are a majority of their employees can't correctly answer the questions. Oh, they might have a general understanding of what it is they do, but for your company to be great and stay great, all employees needs to know the EXACT answer to these questions.

Usually, when you ask somebody what it is they do, they will give you their job title; I am the Director of Human Resources, I am the Head Foreman, I'm the Assistant Director of the Accounting Department, the Head Chef, the Assistant Chef, Director of Purchasing, secretary, receptionist, or cashier. If you expect your company to survive and thrive in any economic environment you need your people to follow that job title statement with a brief paragraph that describes exactly what it is they do.

Let's take the entry level (not really critical or important) position of a receptionist. I mean, so many people might say, all they are really needed to do is just answer the phone; right? I don't see it that way at all. Great companies see a receptionist as the gatekeeper of their company and, a great deal of the time, the receptionist is the first person a customer comes in contact with. Why in the world would you spend thousands, or even millions of dollars on advertising, and then have an incompetent, unmotivated, boring personality person answer your phone?

The old adage, **you don't get a second chance to make a good first impression** comes into play "BIGTIME" when looking at the importance of the receptionist. People love to feel needed, useful and especially … IMPORTANT. In explaining the receptionist's job description to them, **you can make them feel all of these.**

Let me show you what I mean about making a receptionist feel needed, useful and important by breaking down their job description on their first day on the job.

Mr./Ms. Receptionist … we are thrilled to have you as part of our team and wanted to give you an overview as to what you will be doing for us, what is expected of you and also how important your position is to the overall success of our company.

First and foremost you are considered an asset to the business image of our company.

You were hired because we feel you possess strong office and technical skills along with being extremely courteous and tactful.

You have made quite an impression on us and we feel confident you will do the same with our clients.

(When I use the word clients/customers, let that also represent potential or future clients/customers as well)

We all see you as the gatekeeper of our company; the person in charge of …

- *Welcoming visitors by warmly greeting them, in person or on the telephone, and answering or referring inquiries*
- *Setting the tone of professionalism with our clients*
- *Passing along critical information to the right people*
- *Making sure a client gets to the right person or department*
- *Ensuring that a client never has to wait or feel neglected*
- *Notifying company personnel of guest arrivals*

Maintaining …

- *security by monitoring logbook and issuing visitor badges*
- *employee and department directories*
- *clean reception area*
- *Follow-up to make sure the message got in the right hands*

I could go on and on, but I think you now get what I am trying to accomplish here. If I was to ask your receptionist what their job was and they told me, *"answering the phones,"* you've got a problem. A company to me is like a like a living, eating, breathing human organism where everything in our body (company) has a function, a reason for being there. Employees can't be confused or unsure of their function.

I will never forget on a TV show a few years back where something "broke" in the house and they said:

"Did you call the guy?"
"What guy?"
"The guy we always call to fix those things."
"We have a guy for that?"
"Sure. We just call the guy and it gets fixed."

People in your company need to know who "the guy" or "the gal" is... who does what, who is responsible for this or that. I have a notebook in my home office divided with tabs for every company we need to call when something breaks in my home along with every bill we have paid them. I know exactly who to call. In most cases, I know what they can or can't do for me.

I don't care what size you company or organization is, your people need to fully understand what it is they do and how that works, serves, and helps the rest of the company. I like things broken down so there is no confusion. I live by a simple rule: **When in doubt ... Spell It Out.**

LINE RAISER:
List all the positions in your company and then write a job description for each of them.
Now ask your people in those jobs to write their own job descriptions and compare what you have written to what they wrote.
The comparisons will show what you need to work on to get a correct job description written.

This applies to all company sizes. So many times I encounter people in very large companies who don't have a specific job description; their company had grown so fast, that matter was overlooked. You don't want two or more people doing the same thing or inputting/ reporting the same data. Redundancy of tasks can be expensive and lead to confusion. By defining job functions you will be able to see the overall work flow of your organization and see how your people work in conjunction with each other.

CAVEAT: This doesn't mean that because that isn't their "job description" that they can't help out if something else is needed. It is just insuring they fully understand their job function. Once they **"fully"** understand their job description it is critical that you **"fully"** prepare, equip, and arm them with the necessary knowledge and skills to perform their job.

At the peak of their expansion, Starbucks was opening seven new stores every day and adding 15,000 employees every week. How did a small coffee shop in Seattle end up with over 17,000 stores and revenues of more than $10 billion, selling $4 coffee in a fancy cup? How did Starbucks build such an incredible organization that has over 135,000 employees? How do they get their new employees to show up on time and excel at delivering exceptional customer service, especially when many of them are young, unskilled, and lacking little if any experience in business? If you knew the answers to those questions, do you think it might help you expand your business, or on a personal level … help you to become more successful? Let me give you just a little insight to their formula for success.

Howard Behar, the former president of Starbucks once said, ***"We're not in the coffee business serving people. We're in the people business serving coffee."*** When your entire business model is built around delivering exceptional customer service, you have got to figure out a way to instill the necessary SELF-DISCIPLINE in your people so they can correctly handle almost any situation. Long lines, complicated orders … and dealing with sometimes angry, mean, and in-a-hurry customers can be a daily routine for an employee at Starbucks. But, the customer and situation I just described can be the norm in a lot of businesses, so why are employees at Starbucks so good at dealing with it?

It all starts with training. Each *first year employee* will spend **over 50 hours** in the classroom and more time at home studying workbooks or conversing with mentors. Starbucks spends hours upon hours **developing powerful habits** to prepare their people for the onslaught of customers. They have found **that following disciplined habits will enable their people to DEAL with almost any challenge they may face.** *(I will be discussing habits in detail further on in my book.)* They focus on life skills and helping them to handle their emotions and show them how to deliver a **BURST of energy, pep, and enthusiasm when dealing with** <u>every</u> **customer.** They role play with them, interact with them, help, guide, nurture, and **SHOW** them how to handle many different SITUATIONS.

Starbucks has spent millions of dollars creating courses that TRAIN their people on not just the steps of the process, but more importantly, on how to **maintain the self-discipline** to *"do it"* every time. One acronym Starbucks uses to help their people is **LATTE.** It stands for *Listen* to the customer, *Acknowledge* their complaint, *Take Action* by solving the problem, *Thank* them, and then *Explain* why the problem occurred.

Starbucks has developed numerous routines for their employees to follow to help them during stressful situations. By developing these routines, they are helping their people create the RIGHT HABITS to serve their customers. **When an employee is PREPARED, EQUIPPED, and ARMED with the RIGHT HABITS to address almost any situation, delivering exceptional customer service becomes easy.**

LINE RAISER:
A burst of
energy, pep, and enthusiasm
will enhance anything you do
and help to Raise Your Line.

CHAPTER 31
Don't Be a Domino Pusher

You can line up DOMINOS in a beautiful pattern and spend hours doing it … but all you have to do to knock them all down is PUSH over the first one *(the lead domino)* and the rest will follow. The same is true about a business. You can spend years and years building up a great business with a super reputation and one employee can cause a customer to never do business with you again. One employee can PUSH a customer the wrong way and run them off … **in other words … they knocked down one DOMINO.** But, could that one upset customer cause other customers to follow them?

In today's society of instant global communication, one upset customer can put the story out over the internet of your **RIP-OFF … AWFUL SERVICE … UNFAIR TREATMENT …** and seriously hurt your business. PUSHING the one DOMINO can sometimes cause a whole lot of DOMINOS to fall … maybe all of them.

My wife and I found out today the appliance repairman who works for the company that has done ALL of our warranty work, tried to pull a fast one on us; a $2,964.00 fast one. Before we spend that kind of money, I think a second opinion is in order. So, we got the name of a really talented repair man who had done work for our neighbor and had him diagnose the problem. He said it would only cost $74.96 to fix the problem. He had it fixed in less than one hour.

We had purchased ALL our appliances for our home from the first repairman's company and they had done ALL the previous small repairs for warranty work … but now they are out of warranty … and **BANG! … time to soak the stupid consumer who has no idea what is wrong.** I don't know much about appliances, but I do know how to dial a phone. I do know how to go on line and get other opinions. I do have neighbors who may have had similar problems. Now, what damage has been done by the first repairman? TRUST has been destroyed. CONFIDENCE in what the first repairman (and his company) say is now a thing of the past.

Will I ever do business with them again? No!

There are a lot of other companies who sell and service appliances.

Will I tell my friends about what happened? You bet I will.

Will they believe me? They sure will.

More customers will be lost because of what happened to just one customer. **Every single day companies PUSH over Dominos (customers) not realizing the potential damage that might be causing.**

LINE RAISER:
Start handling every customer like they are that
Lead Domino
**who can possibly knock them all down.
If you handle your customers with the
care and honesty they deserve, then you won't have to worry
about other dominos falling (customers leaving).**

Your customers aren't obligated to do business with you. **You need to assume your customers are always teetering, swaying, wavering ... getting ready to fall over (go somewhere else) if you push them the wrong way** ... and on their way down they might just knock over some other dominos (customers) as well.

Are there any DOMINO PUSHERS in your company?
You better hope not because,
they are sure to cause your Profit Line to fall.

CHAPTER 32
The Latest and the Greatest

I recently made it down to the final cut to speak for a Fortune 500 company. Then I received the call they had chosen another speaker over me because of a word I used in my video demo. It wasn't a curse word, a crude remark, a sexist term, an ethnic, racist, or religious slur. In the opinion of this meeting planner, the word I had spoken was an out-dated term. I guess by using this out-dated word I was showing that I wasn't with it, cool, or on the cutting edge of the latest and greatest "fad" in management.

The term I used was *"paradigm."* She was right, the word does have a little age on it. Paradigm first appeared in English in the 15th century, coming from the late Latin word paradīgma, and from the Greek word paradeigma; meaning "an example or pattern," and it still bears this meaning today. Since the 1960s, paradigm has also been used in science to refer to a theoretical framework, as when Nobel Laureate David Baltimore cited the work of two colleagues stating they had *"really established a new paradigm for our understanding of the causation of cancer."* Dictionary.com also gives the definition as, *"a set of assumptions, concepts, values, and practices that constitutes a way of viewing reality for the community that shares them, especially in an intellectual discipline."*

In our quest to stay up with the latest and greatest technology, when just as soon as we pull it out of the box the "techno gadget" is out of date, I feel we are losing sight to some really important concepts, values, and principles in making a company successful.

The latest "management fad" isn't going to make your company successful. Old words like service, trust, respect, loyalty, diligence, fairness, and integrity should never be overlooked in our quest for the latest and greatest technological business tool or management book.

This meeting planner would probably have said of Plato, Socrates, Confucius, Benjamin Franklin, Og Mandino, and Dale Carnegie – *"Yeah they're good, but what have they written lately."*

In between the business transitions from Total Quality Management to Business Process Reengineering (BPR), to Six Sigma to Lean Sigma, don't lose sight of some good old out-dated words. **Service, trust, respect, loyalty, diligence, fairness,** and **integrity** have served me well in my career even though I am still trying to break away from old paradigms which could be holding me back. Oops, I said it again.

But, the flip side to this train of thought is will you have to stay up on the latest and greatest methods of communication if you intend to stay in touch with your customers. Keeping your message out there where it can be seen and heard is just as important as **service, trust, respect, loyalty, diligence, fairness,** and **integrity.**

In simple terms … you better Get Connected or Pull the Plug.

Social media networks are no longer a novelty as they were several years ago. They are mainstream and highly accepted ways of sending and receiving "STUFF" … good stuff, bad stuff, dumb stuff, silly stuff, worthwhile stuff, and pretty useless stuff … all delivered in a blink of an eye.

Companies are no longer being judged by their brick and mortar structures … they are being judged by their websites and Facebook pages. Every day there are over 800,000 more websites and NOW … websites are being reconfigured to (better) fit mobile tablets and phones rather than desktop computers. Why? Because the key factor to what is driving the social web is mobile devices; the number of people accessing the internet via a mobile phone increased by 60.3% to 818.4 million in the last 2 years.

Every 60 seconds ... 41,000 people make a post on Facebook ... there are 2 million searches on Google ... 204 million emails are sent ... 11,000 professional searches are made on LinkedIn ... 216,000 photos sent out over Instagram ... and 278,000 tweets on Twitter. (source: Qmee) **All of these numbers will increase every day.**

You may not like it, nor fully understand it … **but let me say it again … you better Get Connected or Pull the Plug on your business because you won't survive.** This year for the first time in my life I did ALL my Christmas shopping ONLINE with almost all shipping charges waived. NO crowds, NO hassles, NO parking problems, and NO tired/irritated/uninformed sales clerks.

Words like quick, fast, simple, easy, painless, and efficient are driving successful companies today. Several years ago, one of my clients, who has since been bought by FedEx, had a great motto …

E Z T D B W
… it stands for …
Easy To Do Business With.

May I suggest you take a page from their playbook and do the same. Social Media is here to stay and a perfect way to help make your company E Z T D B W (*Easy To Do Business With*).

Companies today are in a constant state of adjustment trying to distinguish the short term fads from the new normal. Just remember this: **Great business principles are a constant, a culture, a fixture for success … everything else is in an ever-moving and evolving state that must be addressed often.**

LINE RAISER:
Never ignore the trends of technology.
If you do, you are setting yourself up
to eventually fail.

CHAPTER 33
Is There a Place for Fairness in Business?

Leon Gorman, the former Chief Executive Officer of L.L.Bean once said: *"Customer service is just a day in, day out, ongoing, never ending, unremitting, persevering, compassionate, type of activity."* In my personal opinion, there is no disputing that statement. We also have to understand that ...

The day we forget
we are in business for the customer
is the day we start going out of business.

So, if the customer is our driving force, it only makes good sense to treat all customers fairly. You would think that point doesn't need to be explained to anyone, but every day, I read about some company totally forgetting that point. Let me give you a prime example of not being FAIR to the customer.

Spirit Airlines made the decision to deny a dying Vietnam War veteran a refund for a ticket he purchased prior to finding out that he would be unable to fly because of his medical condition. The episode went viral on the internet and turned into a glorified PR mess for Spirit Airlines.

I heard an attorney explain that the decision was made for legal reasons because Spirit Airlines did not want to set a precedent that they would refund airfares, for any reason. Wow, if that is the best they can do to explain why they did what they did, what a shame. Only after an enormous uprising of upset people *Tweeting* and *Facebooking* and the news media jumping in, only then, did the CEO finally give in and do what should have been done in the first place. It is really sad it took an uprising to get Spirit Airlines to finally do the right thing. It shouldn't have to be that way.

Are gestures of compassion, caring, concern, charity, grace, empathy, generosity, mercy, kindheartedness, and fairness inappropriate for companies? Have they lost their place in the business world? I think not. I think companies like Southwest

Airlines, Zappos, Nordstrom, Starbucks, Amazon, L.L.Bean, Apple, and USAA *(all listed as top companies in customer service)* would have handled it differently. **I wouldn't want to work for a company that chose precedent over what's right, and I sure don't want to do business with them.**

I think we as consumers respond to companies who do the right thing, go the extra mile, work hard at helping, pleasing, assisting, understanding and searching for better ways to make the customer experience special.

Going above and beyond to help the customer should be engrained in all employees; it should be your corporate culture. A Ritz Carlton employee can spend up to $2,000 without getting corporate approval to help satisfy an upset customer. Now, that is a perfect example of putting the customer first, empowering your employees, and also creating the right corporate culture, all rolled up into one policy.

Is there a place for fairness in business? You bet there is!

Great leaders and great companies understand this principle. For companies to be able to withstand all the trials of a bad economy, all the difficulties of fighting off competitors, and everything else thrown at them, they need to have a strong foundation of character; they need to be known for doing what is fair and honorable for their customers, as well as their employees. Talented, upstanding people want to work for those types of companies and consumers like to do business with them. It should never take an uprising to make a company do what is right.

One of your greatest forms of advertising is your customers. They will talk about your fairness. They will spread the word to others to do business with you because you are fair.

LINE RAISER:

Share stories / examples of fairness
with your employees
that your company has done.

Let your people understand
that your entire organization,
your corporate culture, and your success
is based on
treating all customers fairly.

Make this part of your training program
with all new employees
and watch your Profit Line Rise!

CHAPTER 34
A "To Do" List for Surviving a Recession

It is not a news bulletin to anyone that we are going to experience good economic times and bad ones. About the only thing good I can say about bad economic times is that they will weed out the weak companies in a hurry. Since you are going to face bad economies, economic downturns, and shifts in consumer spending, I thought you might like to have a few suggestions on how to operate in tough times.

➢ First and foremost, forget the **good ole days**, they're gone. Start looking for anything positive to hang your hat on and spread the word.
➢ Regardless of what is going on around you, keep smiling. Always realize your people are watching you and you are setting the tone for how things are going.
➢ Eliminate excess. Have a meeting with your people and ask them what could be eliminated. All special perks are gone, especially those for top management.
➢ Everyone on salary should all come to work a little earlier and stay a little later. This extra time in the office or out selling can really add up in a hurry.
➢ Always be asking your people, *"What do you think,"* and then listen for some possible great ideas.
➢ If you have to say something negative – Don't! Always be positive!
➢ Keep saying to everyone, *"This too will pass."*
➢ Every day prospect, prospect, and prospect some more for new clients and drop by and see how things are going with existing clients – double your contact with them.
➢ Network all the time. Attend more meetings where your customers are going. Think of any way you can cross paths with people who could use your product or service.
➢ Stay visible with your management, associates, and employees. Let everyone see you out and about working on making things better.
➢ Simplify all procedures and paperwork.

- ➤ Ask young people their opinion because they won't say … *"That's the way we've always done it."*
- ➤ Develop strong vendor relationships.
- ➤ Get familiar with everyone in your company and have your managers do the same. Camaraderie is powerful.
- ➤ Respect and appreciate your people. Public recognition is extremely motivating.
- ➤ Receive all customer complaints with thanks and you may even want to consider sending them a gift for those who really spent some time pointing out what you did wrong.
- ➤ Address failures as a learning experience and move on. *"Fail Forward Fast."*
- ➤ Keep asking your people …*"What do we do around here that is stupid, ridiculous, a waste of time or non-productive,"* and then quit doing it/them … now!
- ➤ Avoid negative people and tell people a negative attitude will not be tolerated.

Make these suggestions part of your every day business practice in good times and bad, because they are all LINE RAISERS.

I would like to share one other thought I found years ago from an anonymous source that think will also help you in surviving a recession.

> **"Excellence can be obtained if you:**
> … care more than others think is wise;
> … risk more than others think is safe;
> … dream more than others think is practical;
> … expect more than others think is possible."

When times seem the darkest remember the last line, *"expect more than others think is possible"* … because guess what … **More Is Possible.** Necessity is the ***Mother of Invention*** and persistence is her fuel. Recessions will end and only the most resourceful, flexible, and determined companies will survive.

CHAPTER 35
The Pace of Change is Accelerating

In the last chapter I gave you some suggestions on what you should do to survive a recession. Many of the things I suggested might be contrary to your way of doing business. If that's the case, it looks like to me, you could be headed for some serious problems, because ...

If you don't like change, you are going to hate extinction.

Some people embrace change. Some people just go with the flow and deal with it only when they have to. Then there are those few, die hard, stubborn, inflexible, obstinate people out there, who are going to fight changing to the bitter end. In today's accelerating pace of technological change, I am finding that if you plan on WINNING, SUCCEEDING, and STAYING ON TOP, you better pay attention to the ever-changing landscape of technology.

Blind devotion to past technologies, methodologies, systems, and procedures is a success killer. The pace of change is accelerating in every industry, every market, and in every facet of our daily lives. Technology is coming at us faster than it ever has. It took over 50 years from the invention of the gasoline car before one quarter of the population in the U.S. had one. The telephone required 35 years to hit the one quarter mark. Then things started getting even faster. The television only took 26 years, personal computers took 16 years, and the cell phone reached that population exposure in just 13 years. Apple sold 10 million of the iPhone 5 in the first two weeks of its release.

In his book, *Critical Path*, futurist R. Buckminster Fuller estimated that it we took about 1,500 years, or until the sixteenth century for our amount of knowledge to double. The next doubling of knowledge took only 250 years, which would be close to the year 1750. By 1900, 150 years later, knowledge had doubled again. The doubling speed of knowledge is now between one to two years. So, if it takes 4 years to get through college, everything that was known to mankind the day the student entered college will be quadrupled when they graduate. That is a rather daunting fact; students are behind before they ever get started. According to IBM, the internet will soon lead to the doubling of knowledge every 12 hours.

With all of the information I have just pointed out, I think it is obvious that for companies and people to succeed, they need to embrace change. We all need to stay curious, flexible, inquisitive, and never satisfied with today's standard of excellence. ***What is considered excellent today may be considered average tomorrow.*** But, never forget the fact that technology is no replacement for staying in touch and caring about your customers and your employees. You can have the most technologically advanced company in your industry but if you lie, break promises, make mistakes, don't meet deadlines, are impersonal, emotionless and unwilling to make any extra effort to help customers or care about your employees … you will fail.

If you look for ways to unite technology with a human, caring touch … everyone will benefit.

Several years ago I found some very interesting and surprising statistics on the internet. I found the information so compelling that I saved the data, knowing there would be times I would be able to use it to help give additional insight on the topic of change. Here are the stats I found to be so amazing:

The year was 1907 …

- ▶ The average life expectancy in the U.S. was 47 years old.
- ▶ Only 14 percent of the homes in the U.S. had a bathtub.
- ▶ Only 8 percent of the homes had a telephone.
- ▶ A three-minute call from Denver to New York City cost eleven dollars.
- ▶ Sugar cost four cents a pound.
- ▶ Eggs were fourteen cents a dozen.

▶ Coffee was fifteen cents a pound.
▶ More than 95 percent of all births in the U.S. took place at home.
▶ There were only 8,000 cars in the U.S
▶ There was only 144 miles of paved roads.
▶ The maximum speed limit in most cities was 10 mph.
▶ The tallest structure in the world was the Eiffel Tower!
▶ The population of Las Vegas, Nevada, was only 30 people!
▶ Crossword puzzles, canned beer, and ice tea hadn't been invented yet.
▶ There was no Mother's Day or Father's Day.
▶ Two out of every 10 U.S. adults couldn't read or write.
▶ Only 6 percent of all Americans had graduated from high school.
▶ The average wage in the U.S. was 22 cents per hour.
▶ The average U.S. worker made between $200 and $400 per year.
▶ Most women only washed their hair once a month and used Borax or egg yolks for shampoo.
▶ Canada passed a law that prohibited poor people from entering into their country for any reason.
▶ The American flag had 45 stars. Arizona, Oklahoma, New Mexico, Hawaii, and Alaska hadn't been admitted to the Union yet.
▶ The five leading causes of death in the U.S. were: 1. pneumonia and influenza 2. tuberculosis 3. diarrhea 4. heart disease 5. stroke.
▶ Ninety percent of all U.S. doctors had no college education. Instead, they attended so-called medical schools, many of which were condemned in the press and the government as "substandard."
▶ A competent accountant could expect to earn $2000 per year,
  a dentist made $2,500 per year,
  a veterinarian $1,500 per year,
  a mechanical engineer about $5,000 per year.

Just try to imagine what it may be like in another 100 years! It staggers the mind. We all get cozy, comfortable, complacent, and content with the ways things are going. Humans are essentially creators of habit. Why change? Things are going just fine. Former CEO of Intel, Andy Grove, once said …

"Only the paranoid survive.
Paranoids believe someone or some force is out to get them."

I don't care how big or how little your company is, it won't survive if you become complacent. How many of the **Top 10 Employers** in the United States that existed in 1960 are still in the Top 10 today? **One!** Prominent names like General Motors, U.S. Steel, Ford, Bethlehem Steel, CBS, and General Dynamics have all fallen off the list; only General Electric made it. But, sometimes it is tough to get management to see that changes need to be made. Occasionally, a little trickery might help to make your point. Back in 1993 *Car and Driver* magazine wrote a short article which describes just such a tale of trickery to make your point. *(I am paraphrasing what was written)*

> Mercedes engineers were lobbying management for *"ZIPPIER"* engines but couldn't get anyone to see the need. The COZY attitude of **"They were Mercedes"** ... **the best of the best, the leader"** was pervasive throughout the company. So, the engineers disappeared with a Benz sedan for a few days and returned with the hood chained shut. They brought management in to listen to the new engine they said was more powerful and *"ZIPPIER"* than anything they had ever built. A few of the top executives raced the car up and down the autobahn and even drove it up into the Alps. They really liked the increased performance and couldn't wait to rush back to see what great advances were under the hood. The engineers unshackled the hood to reveal a BMW engine. Management then decided it was time to revamp their motors; it was time to **Raise Their Line**.

Feeling COZY in business is deadly. Don't you ever forget someone is always after your market share and is willing to do **new and different things** to get it. If I told you that right now, your competition is in a meeting, figuring out your weak points and devising a plan to attack you in your most vulnerable points ... what would you do about it?

LINE RAISER:
Constantly be looking for what changes
need to be made to the engine driving your business.

CHAPTER 36
Never Limit Your Sources for Good Ideas

I do lots of strategic planning sessions for companies and I find one of the toughest things to accomplish is to get people to change: to let go of old habits, old procedures, old policies, old rules, or old techniques. The expression ***"That's the way we have always done it,"*** doesn't mean that we should keep on doing it that way. So many procedures just seem to have a life of their own, and just won't die.

Let's say we are all in a meeting and I ask you the following question: ***"Which is better to use for eating ... Chopsticks or Cutlery (fork, knife, spoon)?"*** ... what would be your answer? But, before allowing you to answer, I tried to influence your answer with the following data.

Chopsticks originated in ancient China in the 3rd century B.C. The word first documented use of the term "cutler" *(referring to cutlery)* appeared in 1297. So, cutlery (fork, knife and spoon) have been around for some time, but don't come close to how long people have been using chopsticks. Chopsticks have been used in China, Vietnam, Taiwan, Korea, and Japan for thousands of years.

There are 13 rules of etiquette for how to use chopsticks if you are Chinese, 7 rules for Taiwanese, 6 for Japanese, 5 for Koreans and 7 for Vietnamese. Approximately 24 billion pairs (let me repeat ... billion) of disposable chopsticks are used each year in Japan. In China, an estimated 45 billion pairs of disposable chopsticks are produced yearly.

By sharing all the information above, have I succeeded in influencing your answer to my question - *which is better to use for eating ... Chopsticks or Cutlery?* Does having several billion people using chopsticks sway your opinion of how you should answer? Are you now thinking about tradition, culture, and heritage, rather than efficiency?

Or maybe a past experience will influence your answer. The word chopstick in Chinese is composed of two characters, and the first character means "fast." The first time I used chopsticks the word "fast" never entered my mind. I wanted to stab that piece of meat, *which is improper etiquette for using chopsticks.* Maybe I would agree with the Chinese on "fast," if they let me stab the food, but stabbing is not allowed. So, give me that fork and let me stab away. I grew up with cutlery, so my opinion is bias and my answer will be influenced by my personal experience.

Another thing that can influence answers and hold people back from answering questions or making suggestions about changing a policy is fear of their boss. Their boss might not like their answer; it could be contrary to how the boss would have answered; so, rather than risk upsetting their boss, they stay silent. Their boss could have written the policy, so suggesting they change the policy their boss wrote might be seen as a direct challenge to their boss's authority, or attack on their competence, or possibly an insinuation of ineptness. Remember what I said in Chapter 11, B.O.S.S. is not supposed to stand for a **Bias, Opinionated, Stubborn, Superior** ... it should stand for **Be, Objective, Sensible, and Supportive**.

Well, hopefully now you are starting to see why it is so difficult to get everyone on the same page when answering questions and making decisions in any company. There are so many different issues that can influence people. If you are thinking about changing, tweaking, enhancing, or eliminating a policy, procedure, rule, method, system, or regulation ... you might want to have everyone read this next suggestion.

LINE RAISER:
When having a meeting to discuss needed changes that have to be made to make your company "better" have all titles, agendas, bias, tenure, gender, culture, and loyalties checked at the door.
You might want to include one person (or several) in the meeting who has no relation, affiliation, or connection to the outcome being decided and hear what they have to say.

But, make sure everyone stays focused on the question being asked. I didn't ask if chopsticks are cheaper to make, easier to make, readily available material to produce them, disposable or not ... I simply asked: *Which is better to use for eating ... Chopsticks or Cutlery?*

Great leaders welcome suggestions and new ideas. Great companies realize that if they are not changing with the times, considering new possibilities and looking for better ways ... they will soon become a distant memory to their customer.

LINE RAISER:
When making a decision,
cut *(like a knife)* to the chase *(the issue)*,
spoon up as much information as you can,
and fork over your unbiased opinions;
then have the courage to decide.
To be able to find new ways −
you have to be willing to give up old ways.

I just said great leaders welcome suggestions and new ideas. Let me add to that statement to give it even more power; they also don't care who the idea comes from. A huge problem in most companies is that management thinks great ideas can only come from people with titles, tenure and experience. Nothing is further from the truth. Remember what I said previously, **anyone can have a good idea.**

But, how can you get your people to be more accepting of each other? Sometimes it helps to be more accepting of people when you have a better understanding of their background, challenges they have encountered, or the environment they grew up in, etc.

See if you can figure out what was the "latest" year the person could be born in, for EVERY point I make in the following paragraph, to be true?

They were born when there were no color televisions, Swanson's frozen meals, Xerox copiers, soft contact lenses, Frisbees, or the contraceptive pill. For a while growing up they had to get by without American Express, Visa or Master Card credit cards, pantyhose, microwave ovens, FM radios, tape decks, CD's, or electric typewriters. As a child they didn't get to go to Pizza Hut, McDonald's, Wendy's, or Arby's for a fast food fix. They had five and dime stores where you could actually buy things for 5 and 10 cents ... The year they were born ice-cream cones, phone calls, and a Pepsi all cost a nickel ... and the term "Rock-n-Roll" did not exist.

The first year of their lives their parents couldn't buy Super Glue, diet soft drinks, hula hoops, Mr. Potato Head, acrylic paint or Valium. Back then "grass" was mowed, "coke" was a cold drink, "pot" was something their mother cooked in and "rock music" was their grandmother's lullaby. "Chip" meant a piece of wood, "hardware" was found in a hardware store and "software" wasn't even a word. The average price of a home was $8,450, gas cost 18¢ per gallon, a loaf of bread was 16¢, and it cost 3¢ to mail a letter. Adults made on average $3,210 per year, and the average price for a car cost $1,510.

So, what was the "latest" year this person could be born in for this to all be true?

a. 1925 b. 1930 c. 1935 d. 1940 e. 1945 f. 1950 g. 1955 h. 1960

Go down to the end of this paragraph to see if you chose the right year. Forget the fact that these poor people had to get along for the majority of their lives without e-mail, Facebook, and Twitter, and anything else associated with the internet and computers ... they also grew up without ATM machines, calculators, Teflon, VCR's, permanent press fabrics, bar-code scanners, halogen lamps.

(the answer is F)

It is a wonder that Jay Leno, Steve Wozniak, Stevie Wonder, Dr. Phil, and Richard Branson made it through those terrible times. No video games to play, or cellphones, digital music, on-line shopping, TV remote controls (*they had to get up and walk across the room to change the channel on the TV*) ... no GPS, jet airplanes or Prozac. How did they ever survive?

And these poor souls say things that just make no sense. Statements like … *"Today's weather will be a **CARBON COPY** of yesterday's."* And they will follow that confusing statement with …

"Could you REWIND that?"	Do what ?
"Hey, ROLL-DOWN the window."	Roll what?
"She HUNG-UP on me."	Hung-up what?
"Don't you TOUCH THAT DIAL."	What's a dial?
"That's the last time I will DIAL that number."	It's that dial thing again.
"Let's FILM the birthday party."	We have no film?
"I'm TAPING the ball-game to watch later."	What tape? Tape What?
"Turn the screw CLOCK-WISE."	Clock-wise in a digital world?

Yes, these poor souls would look confused if you told them their Kodak Moment was a Digital Nanosecond. BUT, you know what, they have a real understanding of how THINGS CHANGE.

Here's a quick comparison of "what things cost" in 1950 vs. what they cost in 2015.

- The average price of a home was $8,450 vs $177,600
- Gas per gallon cost 18¢ vs $2.91
- A loaf of bread 16¢ vs $2.25
- To mail a letter cost 3¢ vs 49¢
- Average income per year $3,210 vs $53,046
- The average price for a car cost $1,510 vs $31,252

Yes, I'd say they have seen their fair share of change and they have learned how to deal with it. Because of that reason alone, they are extremely suited to help their younger associates deal with change.

They understand that sometimes
it takes a while before any change will feel right.

So, the next time you have an older person in your group, on your team, assigned to your crew ... get excited about the wealth of knowledge they have actually experienced and go to school on them. And, for you older ones out there, you too, need to get excited if you have some young folks on your team. WHY? Because they understand electronic communication devices better than you ever will, see technology as an advantage, think of possibilities rather than problems, and think the phrase "Why Not" is a call to action.

You need to pay less attention to the way people say things, how they look, how old or young they are, what school they did or didn't graduate from, and base their ideas on merit. You should never base anyone's intelligence or wisdom on the number of wrinkles they do or don't have on their face.

Never allow anyone's age, gender, tenure, race, or experience taint the potential of their ideas.

What if you were in a meeting where a 23 year old, unmarried mother of two children, who only had a high school education (*she received her GED – she did not actually graduate with her class*), and had only been working for your company for less than one year ... suggested that she could do her job just as efficiently from her home. Let's look at her qualifications again:

Education	GED
Age	Extremely young
Time with company	Less than one year
Management experience	None
Knowledge of industry	Limited
Knowledge of business	Very little
Training	2 weeks

I know there are lots of managers out there, if they knew her qualifications, would be wondering who let this person speak. They would be thinking she doesn't have a clue about what she is talking about. Really? According to research done by *Cisco Connected World Report* and *Microsoft* on working remotely from home, they found:

▶ 62 percent of employees believe they could fulfill their job duties at a remote location.

▶ 60 percent of employees believe they don't need to be in the office to be productive and efficient.

That high school educated, young, inexperienced, and unwed mother of two children made a statement that is supported by Microsoft. How can that be? Well, first and foremost, she didn't get caught up in the conventional way of doing things. She simply looked at the things she needs to get her job done.

Maybe management needs to take a step back and not be so judgmental. Maybe you don't have a clue what makes this lady tick. What if you knew she had been deeply in love with a Marine and made a mistake and got pregnant in high school and had to drop out. What if you found out she was an honor student in high school and had qualified for an academic scholarship for college, but gave it up to have the baby. What if you found out that it wasn't one child, but twins she gave birth to. And to top it off, her Marine got killed in Afghanistan on his first deployment one week before being sent home. Would you think differently about her now?

But, I know for a fact that I still have some naysayers out there. *They are still thinking she doesn't have any experience. They are thinking it won't work because you can't have control of your people. They won't get things done without a supervisor looking over their shoulder every once in a while making certain they are working.*

You might want to know that Jet Blue has hundreds of reservation agents operating from their own home. Their home based agents save, on average, up to $4,000 on their commuting expenses, not counting the cost savings of eating out for lunch, daycare, and wardrobe. *The agent could be sitting there in their robe and house slippers and the customer would never know it.*

Jet Blue found they had a 25% increase in productivity once employees were allowed to work from home; Jet Blue figured out a different, more productive, less expensive, more profitable way to operate. Now, what do your think of the suggestion that young, inexperienced mother made?

LINE RAISER:
Never allow anyone's age, gender, tenure, race or experience
taint the potential of their ideas.
Great ideas can come from anyone.
No advancement was ever made by saying,
"That's the way we've always done it."
Figure out a way to involve "the doers" of the task
rather than just the managers of "the doers"
when seeking ideas for improvement.

If you limit your resources for ideas, you limit your ability to Raise Your Line.

CHAPTER 37
The Power of "Re"

The last two chapters hopefully have opened your eyes to the need for addressing change and how to go about doing it. Earlier in the book I told you it was okay to change your mind. To refresh your memory I stated, ***"You must realize and understand that smart people and effective managers are the ones who are willing to CHANGE THEIR MIND and move on. Stubbornness and inflexibility can kill a company and a career."***

I have already identified that change is accelerating around you in every aspect of your business and personal life. Changes or adjustments, whatever word your want to use, are required if you plan on surviving. So, now I want to give you one additional tool to help you be more accepting of all these changes and adjustments you will be making in your career, or in running your business, managing your department, directing your team, or simply influencing your employees and associates.

Let's say a decision was made and the results weren't what you were expecting. Okay, that didn't work so it is now time to try something different. Don't get caught up in the failure of the previous attempt. You now have new data as to what went wrong and you can make adjustments and then try again. That is all I want you thinking about, fixing what didn't work and then ***"do it over differently"*** ... ***"start again differently"*** ... it's a ***"second chance"*** ... a ***"REDO."***

I started thinking about the word **REDO**. The prefix **"RE"** means ***to do again***. So, you have the power of the word "DO," which is the core of all accomplishments, combined with the added safety net of "RE" ... *do it again*.

The tool, concept, methodology, and habit I want you to permanently plant in your mind is the power of "RE." If people would get in the habit of using "RE" more often, things would work out a lot better for them. Get over the fact that whatever you did didn't work. It is time to pull "RE" out of your management toolbox and let it start working for you. One of the definitions for the word tool is: ***anything used as a means of accomplishing a task or*** *purpose.* "RE" will do exactly that. If things aren't going the way you want, then you need to …

RE- flect	RE- think
RE- build	RE- establish
RE- view	RE- generate
RE- new	RE- structure
RE- vise	RE- organize
RE- direct	RE- capture
RE- work	RE- cover
RE- fine	RE- arrange
RE- do	RE- evaluate
RE- form	RE- tract
RE- start	RE- create

Now, there are some people out there who will immediately take the opposite point of view on "RE." They will RE-fuse any advice. They will RE-frain from changing anything. They will RE-sist and RE-sent any suggestions you give. So, they will keep RE-peating their past mistakes and RE-linquish any chance they have for future success. Their choice of how they look at "RE" will RE-veal who they really are; they are a failure getting ready to happen.

LINE RAISER:

Quit being so RE-luctant in RE-doing something.
Just admit it didn't work out, RE-lax and move on.
Quit living with RE-morse or RE-gret
and RE-claim a positive outlook.
RE-energize yourself, RE-coup your self-esteem
and RE-ject any notion that you can't
RE-gain what has been lost … and make it even better.

Welcome to the POWER of "RE."
When you RE-fuse to be defeated you RE-lease the power
to RAISE YOUR LINE.

SECTION 4

Raising Your Line Personally

CHAPTER 38
Personal Pep Talk

Most of us seldom get to hear a great Pep Talk. The great coaches, Presidents, generals, business icons ... "LEADERS" ... don't happen to be at our "beckoning" to fire-us-up. No, we are all pretty much left on our own when it comes to preparing ourselves for the ... encounters, surprises, conflicts, setbacks, struggles, and tasks we face every day. Some people start their day with one or more of the following things on their mind:

- feeling underpaid
- thinking their skills are underutilized
- dreading the commute to work
- thinking their job is mundane/unimportant/mediocre
- hating the long hours
- loathing the office atmosphere and work culture
- disliking some of their coworkers
- abhorring the unnecessary meetings
- extremely annoyed that their boss plays favorites
- upset that they are not allowed any creativity in their job
- seething that they are not recognized for their hard work and dedication

I got depressed just writing that ... so think how tough it must be on folks who have to face it EVERY DAY.

We even have expressions we throw out which are meant to be positive, that really are addressing our inner feelings of dealing with the drudgery of work. **"HUMP DAY!"** Which really means ... thank goodness, the week is half over. Then we close out the week with **"TGIF"** – the acronym for **"Thank God it's Friday,"** which the Urban Dictionary defines as: Used to express the joy one feels in knowing that the work week has officially ended and that they have two days off with which to enjoy.

I don't care what your frame of mind is when you wake up in the morning, because I believe there is a way to better prepare you for the day and help you handle whatever is in store for you. I have been doing it for several years and it works for me, so I thought I would share this simple habit I have developed with you.

> # LINE RAISER:
> **Every morning, read at least 10 minutes of nothing but motivational, inspirational, or personal development quotes "BEFORE" you get on with your work for the day.**

When I sit down at my desk ... it's the first thing I do. Remember, the objective is to prepare you for what you are getting ready to encounter, so it is imperative that you read the quotes first. Don't listen to voicemail, or check your emails, texts, or Facebook. First, get your mind "RIGHT" for the day. To some of you this may sound corny, stupid, silly, or simply a waste of time ... but for me ... it works. It really helps jump-start my day, fires me up and puts me in a positive frame of mind ... which is not a bad way to start any day. Some great examples of quotes that have helped me are:

"Welcome the task that makes you go beyond yourself."
Frank McGee

"Failure is simply the opportunity to begin again, this time more intelligently."
Henry Ford

"No one can make you feel inferior without your consent."
Eleanor Roosevelt

LINE RAISER:

If you are a manager, have a "quote project" with
your employees. Have them come up with their favorite
personal development and/or success quotes –
then figure out a way to share them with everyone.
You might even want to consider having a
"Quote of the Day" email you send out.

There are countless ways you can run with this that will be beneficial for all involved. I think the late, great motivational speaker Zig Ziglar explained it best when he said, ***"People often say that motivation doesn't last. Well, neither does bathing – that's why we recommend it daily."*** Do whatever you have to do to start making **"A Personal Pep Talk"** part of your daily routine.

If we spend time reading Great Thoughts –

We will be planting the seeds to Create Great Things.

Getting yourself fired up is also a great way to feel good about yourself. Who should be your biggest fan? **You!** If you don't think you are good, why should anybody else? I believe one of the biggest mistakes we make in trying to improve is getting down on ourselves and staying there. Self-doubt is a proven "killer" to accomplishment. You will be a lot better off BELIEVING you can do something rather than DOUBTING that you can do it.

First and foremost, we need to address the difference in being confident in your abilities compared to being a vain, arrogant, conceited, cocky, pompous, stuck-up, egotistical, narcissistic, self-loving jerk. You don't need to go around singing your own praises and telling everybody just how wonderful you are. But, you also don't need to be so meek and timid that no one ever calls on you to lead the group or solve the problem or give your opinion because you have never shown an ounce of confidence in anything you do. If you just blend in with the office decor, you will never succeed.

Success comes to those who take it, not to those who hope it comes. You constantly need to be preparing, studying, and learning, so when an opportunity presents itself … you can deliver. That being said, sometimes you need to "step up" and let people know you can do it. Start believing you can do it. Start seeing yourself as talented, smart, and resourceful. Just how smart are you? Compared to the people listed next … you are looking brilliant.

■ A lady called into a talk radio station to complain about where the department of transportation places **"Deer Crossing"** signs. She thought it was stupid that they placed the signs in such high-traffic areas and felt there would be fewer accidents *(hitting the deer)* if they moved the signs to less congested traffic areas. She actually believed the deer were paying attention to the signs as to where they could cross. You can hear exactly what she had to say by going to … www.youtube.com/watch?v=CI8UPHMzZm8.

■ A person called the warranty department of a computer manufacturer and explained that the "cup holder" on their hard drive broke. The technician explained to the customer that their computer did not come with a cup holder. The technician finally realized that the customer was using the CD drive (in the eject position) to hold their coffee cup.

■ Another large computer company has considered changing the instructions of "press any key" to read "press the return key" because so many customers have called their customer service help line saying … they can't find the "ANY" key.

■ A councilman in Washington, D.C. once stated, *"If crime went down 100% it would still be fifty times higher than it should be."*

■ And to really make you feel smart … The following questions have actually been asked by attorneys in a court of law.

> ➤ *"How many times have you committed suicide?"*
> ➤ *"Were you present in court this morning when you were sworn in?"*
> ➤ *"You don't know what it was, and you didn't know what it looked like, but can you describe it?"*

I don't know about you, but I'm feeling smarter already. In all seriousness, the sooner you start having a more positive outlook on your self-worth, the better you'll be. Even if you are just starting out or starting over in a new career, those with confidence will go the furthest. You have got to understand those with confidence SUCCEED, and those with doubt, FAIL.

William Shakespeare said, ***"Our doubts are traitors, and make us lose the good we oft might win, by fearing to attempt."*** Self-doubt is a lack of faith or confidence in oneself and is a common reason for failure in just about everything we do. Everyone, at some time in their life has experienced it and then had to deal with the fear, anxiety, worry, and for some, even panic that comes with self-doubt.

Will it work, am I good enough, will I make the shot, what if I forget my lines, they won't like me, I'm not ready, I'm from the wrong side of the tracks, if I miss the field goal we will lose, what if I trip ... the list of self-doubts is endless.

Let's get one thing straight, self-doubt is natural. Having self-doubt doesn't mean you are weak or weird. It can creep into the minds of the greatest athletes, musicians, doctors, and business people, regardless of how successful they have been. You need to never underestimate its destructive power, because if left unchecked, it can cause us to quit, lose, fail, or radically compromise our hopes and dreams.

So ... how do we overcome self-doubt? The way to overcome self-doubt is to take action. Taking action, doing, trying and then trying again builds confidence; confidence builds courage and courage kills self-doubt. Aerodynamically the bumblebee shouldn't be able to fly but someone forgot to tell it that. You need to eliminate unproductive thinking and take the leap. The worst thing that can happen is you learned something from the experience and have an even better chance to succeed the next time.

Have I ever been nervous? Yep! Were my hands sweating? Yep! Did I have an uneasy feeling in my stomach? Absolutely! Had I ever felt that way before? Yes ... many times. Over the years I have learned to realize that everything I was feeling was NATURAL. In fact, I learned I could use those feelings to my advantage. I found that because my adrenalin was pumping, my senses were peaked, my mind was clear and more focused ... my body was getting ready to take on the challenge.

Scottish philosopher Thomas Carlyle once said, *"Doubt, of whatever kind, can be ended by action alone."* Self-doubt is a feeling of uncertainty; an insecurity that can lead to hesitation and indecision. You eliminate the feeling when you dispel the cause. Start answering the simple questions; are you ready ... have you prepared properly ... do you know what you are supposed to do like you know your own name? If you can answer *"Yes"* to those questions, then it is time to take action.

The great American industrialist Henry Ford stated, *"The man who thinks he can and the man who thinks he can't are both right."* So, throw out the second part of Mr. Ford's sentence; prepare, study, practice and realize that those scared, anxious, uneasy feelings means your body is gearing up to help you do something special ... Now Go For It!

If you don't believe in yourself why should anyone else believe in you?

LINE RAISER:
Don't ever let self-doubt stand between where you are and where you want to be.

CHAPTER 39
B.O.U.N.C.E

Okay, you've got the right attitude, you are fired up for the day and then, BOOM, something bad happens. Nothing is worse than that moment you realize you have been fooled, or been taken advantage of, used, abused, betrayed, misled, or lied to. I have always found that you need to have an alternative, a back-up plan, a second approach ... just in case the unexpected happens ... so you can regroup, **BOUNCE** back, and move on.

There is an old poem (1785) by Robert Burns, which John Steinbeck used to name his highly acclaimed book *Of Mice and Men* (1937) that addressed *things not going the way we had planned*. Bringing the poem and book up to current times, what both men were addressing is ... **the best-laid plans often go awry. The most carefully prepared plans may go wrong.** No matter how much thought, time, and effort you put into it .... something can still go wrong. **Everything you do is subject to outside forces that can alter, change, or disrupt** your planned outcome.

"Things Happen" ... "Stuff Happens" ... "It Happens"

When my son, Tyler, was in grad school, he had been promised some things that we had no reason to doubt would happen. Then, out of the blue, things changed. Promises were altered, facts became variables, and the variables now affected outcomes. When he told me what had happened, I told him not to worry ... we had never counted on those promises and we had a back-up plan. It was interesting watching the evolution of maturity taking place in his mind as this situation unfolded. He now had seen how critical having a back-up plan was. He had also witnessed how ... *not everything had been disclosed to him.* He learned a great lesson, but more importantly, he was able to **BOUNCE** back and move on in another direction.

Walt Disney was laid off and told he had no drawing ability and also went bankrupt before **BOUNCING** back and creating his vast empire. Abraham Lincoln, Henry Ford, Donald Trump and ketchup magnate, H.J. Heinz, also went bankrupt and **BOUNCED** back. The legendary actor and comedian of the golden age of Hollywood, George Burns, made fourteen films and then hit a rough spot ... a thirty-seven year rough spot. Then he received an offer to appear in the movie *The Sunshine Boys*. He **BOUNCED** back and won an Oscar for his role at the age of 80. He kept working until he was 98 years old.

No one is exempt from having
bad things happen to them.
"Bad" has no boundaries;
bankruptcy, failure, mistakes, wrong decisions,
setbacks, illness, poor choices, gaffes, errors,
slip-ups, disappointments, and blunders
can happen to anyone.
The difference between those who succeed
from those who don't has a great deal to do with
if and how they **BOUNCE** back
when things go wrong.
Make the following acronym for B.O.U.N.C.E.
part of your strategy for success:

B.O.U.N.C.E.

BEGIN OVER UNDERSTANDING NEW CHOICES EXIST

Now, I am not making light of BOUNCING back. Sometimes you get the wind knocked right out of your sails and moving on almost seems like an impossibility. A dear friend sent me a portion of an article that had some interesting references to Easy vs. Hard. The unknown author was relating how … ***bad is easy - good is hard …*** ***losing is easy - winning is hard … talking is easy – listening is*** ***hard.*** There were numerous comparisons of Easy vs. Hard and I thought I would share some of them with you because the examples will really make you think:

EASY   vs   HARD

➤ Arguing is easy.   Negotiating is hard.
➤ Play is easy.   Work is hard.
➤ Giving advice is easy.   Taking advice is hard.
➤ Falling is easy.   Getting up is hard.
➤ Cowardice is easy.   Bravery is hard.
➤ Borrowing is easy.   Paying back is hard.
➤ Poor is easy.   Rich is hard.
➤ Lying is easy.   Truth is hard.
➤ War is easy.   Peace is hard.
➤ Sarcasm is easy.   Sincerity is hard.
➤ Criticizing is easy.   Taking criticism is hard.
➤ Holding a grudge is easy.   Forgiving is hard.
➤ Following is easy.   Leading is hard.
➤ Eating is easy.   Dieting is hard.

I believe success comes to those people who learn how to do the hard things. They accept them for what they are: **difficulties they** **must handle if they plan on being successful.** It is easier to win when you are prepared. Negotiating is simpler when you are open-minded. Peace makes more sense when you understand the ravages of war. Telling the truth is better when you have seen the damage lying will do to a reputation. If you believe criticizing others is helpful, then why shouldn't it be helpful when they criticize you? Those who "HANDLE THE HARD" deserve the rewards it brings. This is what separates the winners from the losers. So, take a different perspective when you encounter life's difficult tasks and start appreciating what you are about to accomplish.

LINE RAISER:

**Realize that by taking on the *Hard Tasks*
you are about to become better,
improve your position,
or refine your skills,
and there is nothing ever wrong with that.**

CHAPTER 40
Get the M.U.D. Out of Your Life

Years ago, Toyota embraced and developed a methodology for identifying and removing inefficiencies and waste in what came to be known as the famous Toyota Production System. Companies worldwide came to their facilities to see just how Toyota was accomplishing such incredible production efficiencies. Toyota had found great success by identifying and eliminating MUDA ... which is the Japanese word meaning "uselessness, pointlessness, inefficiency, disorganized, futility, idleness, and wastefulness."

I believe we can take some points from Toyota's manufacturing methodology to help us personally become better. Just as there are inefficient, pointless, useless, wasteful things done in manufacturing, I think the same is true about how we manage our daily lives. I decided to alter the word MUDA just a bit, so it would more appropriately represent something we can all relate to. I want MUDA to be replaced with the acronym M.U.D. ... which stands for Meaningless, Unnecessary, Distractions. The reason I chose M.U.D. is because I have never had much use for it.

- Mud clogs things up.
- You get it on your car and you want to wash it off.
- You get it on your shoes and you want to wipe it off.
- You can get stuck in the mud when walking or driving.
- You track it into your house and you have to clean it up.
- It gets on your car windshield and you can't see to drive.
- You can't see in muddy water and you sure don't want to drink muddy water.

Yes, I can personally say I have never had any need for mud in my life. I feel the same is true if we want to become and remain successful ... we have no need for **Meaningless, Unnecessary, Distractions**. I believe we can use this simple acronym **(M.U.D.)** as the identifier and symbol for what is holding us back.

Every time we encounter M.U.D. we need to clean it up, remove it, and eliminate it from ever coming back … if at all possible.

M.U.D. is everywhere in our lives … phone calls, the Internet, e-mails, texting, Facebook, Twitter, YouTube, Social Media, gossiping, television, co-workers, advertisements … yes, M.U.D. is being slung at us from all directions and stealing valuable time we can never get back. The first key in eliminating M.U.D. from our lives is to see, realize, understand, and RECOGNIZE things that are Meaningless, Unnecessary, Distractions. Let me give you one simple example:

> You are at your desk and want to look something up on the Internet. You click on your computer and go to your main page and before you type into the Google bar what you are looking up … you take a moment to read a headline off your main page … which in turn might cause you to take more time because you read the article under the headline. Welcome to M.U.D. But, only you can see it as M.U.D.; only you can make the decision not to get dirty (slowed down) with this M.U.D.

I am doing everything I can to clean up the M.U.D. in my daily life. I have found that mental distractions only delay us in reaching any goal we desire. The great ones know to never let that which does not matter affect the things that do matter.

If you want to Raise Your Line, eliminate the M.U.D. in your life.

CHAPTER 41
Opinions

The other day I read an article about a person that I had recently met and worked with several months prior. This individual is at the top of his profession and everyone wants to know "The Secret," "The Magic," or "The Formula" to his success. He is inundated with requests for interviews, speaking engagements, and public appearances. Unfortunately, he has very little time to devote to such requests if he is to maintain his success and still have some time left to be with his family. But, he relented to a request for a big article and allowed the writer a great deal of access to him over several weeks.

In my humble opinion, I found the article to be a mean and unfair depiction of this individual that will forever taint the OPINION of those who will never meet ... much less ... ever get to know this person. The point I am trying to make is that OPINIONS are like "Butts" ... everyone has got one ... though they do come in all shapes and sizes. You've got pretty ones, ugly ones, fat ones, skinny ones, bouncy ones, tight ones, strong ones, and weak ones ... but we've all got one. Just because we have one, doesn't make us an expert on the subject of butts ... derriere, bootie, bottom, tush, cheeks, buns, fanny, behind, rear end, rump, gluteus maximus ... or Forest Gump's descriptive term, "The Buttocks."

I feel we all need to be extremely cautious when it comes to accepting the OPINIONS of others about people we have never met. Magazine editors might be more interested in selling magazines than in giving a true assessment of the person their journalists are writing about. Sensationalism is a type of editorial bias in mass media to increase readership numbers. The title alone can prove extremely hurtful and misleading, along with instantly and wrongly labeling the person being written about.

Just as sensational headlines sucker us into accepting false premises, we must not let other people's OPINIONS establish false premises about individuals. Unless the OPINION is coming from someone you trust and have known for years, who has no axe to grind, no agenda, no reason to bear false witness ... always be cautious as to what you accept as fact about anyone. I have found that many times if someone isn't who we want them to be, we get annoyed. If we can't understand how they are so good at what they do … we get angry, irritated, envious, and/or bitter. There are a lot of people out there who seem to have a clear idea of how other people should lead their lives … and will share their OPINION about that … yet they don't have a clue how to live their own life.

Some people might think that the actions of a focused person are rude. Other people might think the actions of a disciplined, dedicated person were conceited, smug, distant, cold, or aloof. What's even worse is that these same people decide who someone else is and share that OPINION, when they don't even know who they are themselves. Just because it is written in the paper, a book, or magazine … or seen on TV or the Internet … doesn't make it true and factual. I have also found that those who gossip a lot seem to get things wrong a lot. If you need to find out what a person is all about, do your OWN RESEARCH.

IF YOU WANT AN OPINION YOU CAN TRUST MAKE IT YOUR OWN

You also need to be very cautious when "THEY" start sharing their opinion with you and the rest of the world. I am really tired of "THEY." "They" said:

- ➢ FedEx was not a feasible business concept.
- ➢ No one will ever run a mile in under 4 minutes.
- ➢ Heavier-than-air flying machines are impossible.
- ➢ The supercomputer is technologically impossible.
- ➢ Ronald Reagan doesn't have that presidential look.
- ➢ Everything that can be invented has been invented.
- ➢ Airplanes are interesting toys but of no military value.
- ➢ A rocket will never be able to leave the Earth's atmosphere.
- ➢ There is no reason anyone would want a computer in their home.
- ➢ The world potential market for copying machines is 5000 at most.

- ➢ The earth is flat.
- ➢ Radio has no future.
- ➢ X-rays will prove to be a hoax.
- ➢ Man will never reach the moon regardless of all scientific advances.

"THEY" said Elvis, The Beatles, Marilyn Monroe, Charles Schultz, and Walt Disney would never make it.

In 1993, "THEY" said IBM, which had just lost $8 billion, was DEAD.

In 1997, "THEY" said that Apple Computer, which was on the verge of bankruptcy, was FINISHED.

The people who said all these WRONG things were considered smart folks ... **but "THEY" got it wrong.**

I wonder what **"THEY"** might possibly say about you ... that will be totally WRONG.

> *"You'll always be a failure."*
> *"You'll never make this team."*
> *"You aren't management material."*
> *"You will never amount to anything!"*
> *"You don't have an innovative bone in your body."*
> *"You won't be able to dig your way out of this mess!"*

I've never been a fan of **"THEY,"** nor should you. *The masses, the simpletons, the opinionated, the condescending, the negative, the intolerant, the pompous, the weak, the short-sighted, the feeble-minded, the narrow-minded ...* have no idea what you are capable of. **"THEY"** have no idea how much desire, tenacity, and willpower you have. You can wake up earlier, go to bed later, study harder, learn, refine, tweak, adjust, improve, perfect, and come back even stronger; **"THEY"** can't stop you.

You don't have to be the smartest person in the room to be enormously successful. **Abraham Lincoln went to war a captain and returned a private.** Think about that. He went to war an Officer and returned with the lowest rank in the military. Now that is bad! Winston Churchill struggled in school and failed the sixth grade. **Henry Ford went broke five times.** Let that number sink in ... **FIVE TIMES**.

So many people I run across today got knocked down hard in our last recession and are still struggling and lamenting over their misfortune. Ford lost it all five times and he still came back — **BIG!** *Let it be noted that "THEY" have gotten it WRONG countless times.*

LINE RAISER:

Always remember that ...
"THEY" have nothing to do with
how good YOU can be.

"THEY" won't make it happen,
YOU WILL.

CHAPTER 42
Eliminating Bad Habits

A HABIT is a recurrent, often unconscious pattern of behavior that is acquired through frequent repetition. The key to success in business and your personal life is eliminating bad habits and developing good habits. The English novelist Charles Reade I think said it best when he wrote:

> "Sow a thought and you reap an act;
> Sow an act and you reap a habit;
> Sow a habit and you reap a character;
> Sow a character and you reap a destiny."

Why is it that some people succeed while others fail or lead lives of mediocrity? Now, I'm not suggesting a life of mediocrity is bad. If that is your aspiration, then so be it. But if you aspire to be something more, then you need the answer to this question: **What do you need to do to be successful?** That answer seems to elude most people. You are where you are today because of your past decisions, and your future is completely in your hands.

The renowned author Oliver Wendell Holmes once said, *"We all need an education in the obvious."* Our problem is sometimes we fail to see, admit and/or identify what is really obvious to others; our bad habits. It has been proven time and time again that successful people are creatures of "good habits." So what could be **holding you back** from reaching your goals is *an education in the obvious;* **NOT identifying your bad habits**. It's your life and you have only got one shot at it; this isn't a dress rehearsal. When it is over, you don't get a redo, so get real and start addressing your bad habits.

This is not a pleasurable task, but it is a highly necessary one if you plan to grow, prosper, and succeed. Over the years in training workshops I have conducted, I have collected a great deal of material on good and bad habits. Let me share with you some of the most common bad habits my attendees have identified:

- ▶ Taking work home with you
- ▶ Socializing too much on the phone
- ▶ Wasting time surfing the Internet
- ▶ Having your cell phone on all the time
- ▶ Not paying off your credit card monthly
- ▶ Shuffling papers on your desk
- ▶ Not having a "Things To Do list"
- ▶ Not following your "Things To Do List"
- ▶ Getting no exercise
- ▶ Wasting time gossiping
- ▶ Lack of defined goals
- ▶ Allowing bills to go unpaid
- ▶ Watching too much television
- ▶ Not enough sleep
- ▶ Not following through on promises
- ▶ Associating yourself with losers

I am just scratching the surface with the list of possible bad habits we all can have. **If you don't like where you are in life, get honest with yourself and start eliminating the things that are holding you back.** The only person who can fix you, is you.

LINE RAISER:
**Have a meeting with yourself and identify your bad habits.
You really need to get honest with yourself.
Come up with at least five and then decide which one
will help you the most if you eliminate it.
Now concentrate on eliminating it.**

So, what is your excuse for not doing this? Benjamin Franklin once said: *"He that is good for making excuses is seldom good for anything else."* Syndicated cartoon columnist, writer and artist Don Wilder had a wonderful description of excuses. He said, *"Excuses are the nails used to build a house of failure."* What a profound description of the value and outcome of an excuse.

What stands between most people and their goals are a bunch of excuses. Now, some people get real fancy and rationalize the situation … thinking they are not giving an excuse. American novelist and philosopher, Ayn Rand, destroyed that notion when she said, *"Rationalization is a process of not perceiving reality, but of attempting to make reality fit one's emotions."* I find people who are good at making excuses, are seldom good at reaching goals, solving problems, and leading people. I am tired of people who say:

- ▶ I can't
- ▶ I won't
- ▶ I should have
- ▶ I meant to
- ▶ I wanted to
- ▶ That's impossible
- ▶ That'll never work
- ▶ That's not my job
- ▶ Life isn't fair
- ▶ I'm too tired
- ▶ I didn't know

- ▶ That's the way we've always done it
- ▶ I just don't have the willpower
- ▶ I knew I shouldn't have
- ▶ I was thinking about doing it
- ▶ I wish I could
- ▶ I need more respect
- ▶ I'm not good enough
- ▶ I'm scared of failing
- ▶ It's too hard
- ▶ I'll never be able to learn that
- ▶ No one told me not to do it

To me, an excuse is a form of weakness or inability to take responsibility for your own mistakes. Excuses usually show a weakness in your plan, or your attitude, your conviction, ability, knowledge, judgment, talent, or organizational skills. But, I also think making an excuse is a sign of cowardice. By making an excuse for your actions, you are showing a lack of courage in accepting the consequences for those actions. Please understand, **excuses may make you feel better, but they change nothing and usually annoy the people you are telling them to.**

I have found that successful managers/bosses/leaders ... when something bad happens, a mistake is made, a goal isn't reached ... would rather you tell them what happen, what you learned and what you are going to do about it, than give them an excuse. **If you are always on the lookout for a great excuse, you better also be on the lookout for a new job.**

Helen Keller was the first blind and deaf person to EVER earn a Bachelor of Arts degree. If there was ever a person who had a great excuse for not being able to graduate from college, I think she should be right at the top of that list. Florence Nightingale, who is known as the founder of modern nursing stated, *"I attribute my success to this - I never gave or took any excuse."* So, the next time you are thinking about giving an excuse – DON'T. **If you quit looking for an excuse – you will have more time to find a solution.**

Now, I ask you —

"What is your excuse for not eliminating your bad habits?"

Okay, so much for having excuses. Now let's get to work on your bad habits. I believe the following poem I wrote on "Bad Habits" will give you a better perspective of what you now need to do.

Bad Habits Staring Back at Me

I looked in the mirror and what did I see,
a person with some bad habits staring back at me.
There are some that are trivial and a tad bothersome at best,
but there are a few that I see standing out from all the rest.

I've thought about them before, no they are not new to me,
but they are still here and they definitely shouldn't be.
What is different about today as I see my reflection looking back,
is a commitment in my heart to change … that I no longer lack.

There are no crowds cheering or coaches to push me on,
becoming a better person is what I will be building upon.
So I made the decision to concentrate on just one,
eliminating that bad habit has just got to be done.

And when that one bad habit is gone and a better person am I,
it will be time to pick one more and give it a try.
For the one truth I know … a very sobering fact,
failure comes from not improving … so now I must act.

Do yourself a favor and take a lesson from me,
we can all be better people … if we just commit to be.
Pick one thing to fix and do it today,
for striving to be better … you should never ever delay.

It's time to commit to eliminating some bad habits. The key word in that last sentence is **COMMIT**. Renowned German writer and statesman, Johann Wolfgang von Goethe, explained his view on the Power of Commitment this way: *"Until one is committed there is hesitancy, the chance to draw back, always ineffectiveness ... Whatever you can do or dream you can, begin it. Boldness has genius, power and magic in it. Begin it now."*

The stories on success are not written about people who said *... "I would've done that ... I could've done that ... I should've done that."* The stories are written about people who have done it. Five hundred millionaires were asked what really caused them to be so successful. Most said, *"I finally decided to get serious."*

Many of those millionaires also said that they had faced their biggest adversity right before becoming successful ... in other words ... they hit rock bottom right before they hit their peak. **You don't want to be a person with PERMANENT POTENTIAL.**

Success is a result of achievement, not good intentions. At the beginning of every year many people make a *New Year's Resolution List:* lose weight, stop smoking, exercise more, learn a second language, lower their cholesterol, spend more time with their family, etc., etc., etc. Making a list is a great idea because *"How do you know you got there, if you don't know where you are going?"* Unfortunately most people never accomplish anything on their list. Why?

There can be many reasons why people fail at achieving their *New Year's Resolutions:* lack of commitment and resolve, poor planning, poor organization, lack of time or poor time management, letting trivial things interfere, choosing too many, depending on others to help, and/or family demands. With all the surprises and demands that pop-up in our daily lives, "New Year's Resolutions" start getting pushed further and further back until they just disappear.

My question to you is, *"Just how badly do you want to be successful?"* You could be thinking that is a silly question; all people want to be successful. If that is true, then something is amiss. Why are there so many people who aren't successful or who never reach their full potential? **I believe it is because they lack the**

commitment and intensity needed to make it happen. Here is a great story to help corroborate the point I am trying to make.

> Socrates was once asked by a young man how he could gain wisdom. Socrates asked the young man to accompany him while he took a stroll around a lake and he would discuss the matter with him. Socrates then asked the lad to follow him into the lake where they were standing in water that was chest deep. This seemed odd to the young man, but who was he to question Socrates. Then all of a sudden, Socrates grabbed the young man and pushed him down until his head was fully submerged under the water and held him there. At first, the young man thought this was just a joke, so he didn't fight back. Socrates held him longer and longer until the lad panicked and started struggling to free himself from Socrates grasp. He was running out of air, his lungs were aching for oxygen, his heart was pounding and his adrenalin was sky-high. Socrates finally released his grasp so the young man could emerge. Gasping for air, panic-stricken from the ordeal, the young man screamed out in a barely audible voice, **"What are you doing?"** Socrates calmly replied,

> **"When you desire wisdom with the same intensity**
> **that you desired to breathe,**
> **then nothing will stop you from getting it."**

I can share with you the wisdom I have learned from the many clients I have worked with. I can put the information in a format that is simple to understand. But, until you have the burning desire to learn, change, adapt, and internalize the information, so it will help to make you more successful, nothing I share will help. To paraphrase Socrates, *"When you have the desire to become successful, with the same intensity that you have to breathe, then nothing will stop you from getting it."* Let's get one thing perfectly clear:

YOU control your destiny by the choices YOU make.

I am going to throw a list of questions at you and let you reflect on your answers. Now, some of these questions might not be applicable to you at all, which is good. BUT, if one or more of these questions strikes a nerve when you read them, then you may have some work to do.

Why do you waste time?
Why don't you rest more?
Why don't you eat better?
Why do you procrastinate?
Why don't you laugh more?
Why don't you forgive more?
Why don't you exercise more?
Why aren't you more efficient?
Why are you so critical of others?
Why don't you save more money?
Why do you waste time listening to gossip?
Why don't you take more time for yourself?
Why are you sometimes or all the time ... late?
Why don't you say what you are really feeling?
Why do you put so much pressure on yourself?
Why do you spend more money than you should?
Why are you sometimes or always in a bad mood?
Why do you sometimes or always doubt yourself?
Why do you stay in a job or relationship you hate?
Why do you say yes when you really want to say no?
Why don't you spend more time with the ones you love?
Why don't you treat everyone with the same respect you want?
Why don't you read something every day that will make you better?
Why don't you tell the people you care about that you care about them?

The REALITY OF YOUR ANSWER to each question is very telling. If the answer to any one of the questions is because YOU have chosen to do so ... then YOU can change it, alter it, or correct it. Quit blaming others for what YOU HAVE CHOSEN. Example: *You will eat better when YOU DECIDE that it is important to your health TO DO SO. But, unfortunately most people wait until they have medical problems and a doctor puts restrictions on their diet before they change their eating habits.* Look at each question and then decide what is important to YOU. Remember what I said earlier: **Your life is not a dress rehearsal. You've got one shot at it, so try and make it your BEST SHOT.**

The day you *REALIZE / ACKNOWLEDGE / ACCEPT* the fact that YOU control your destiny by the choices YOU make is the day you start taking control your life.

You have probably heard what I am getting ready to say hundreds of times, but I think it is very appropriate to bring it up again right now. **Today is the first day of the rest of your life ...** so how are you **NOW** going to approach "your first day" with all that I have just said about habits?

The alarm rings and it's another day. Most of the time we go about it with the same routine; from working out to when you have breakfast, coffee, paper reading time, and commute to the office ... you get the picture ... SOSDD (Same Old Stuff Different Day). I am not one for messing with a good routine, but I am one for trying to figure out ways to get better.

The other day I ran across an idea from the CEO of Zappos (The Internet Shoe Store) who took his company from $0.00 in sales to $1 billion in less than ten years and then sold it to Amazon for over $1.2 billion in 2009. He said that they try to make at least one improvement in their organization every week, but suggests on a personal basis to shoot for some sort of improvement daily. He went on to say, *"Wake up every day and say to yourself what is the 1% improvement I can do to make myself better both personally and professionally."* Now you're thinking, *"Rob, where in the world am I going to find the time to make this 1% improvement goal work?"* ... well let me help you with that.

Found 5 minutes -   Streamline your morning routine time to dress, shave, put on makeup, drink coffee, read the paper, etc., or just get up 5 minutes earlier.

Found 5 minutes - Avoid idle talkers, gossiping or other distractions. If your conversation is not a constructive one, get out of it.

Found 10 minutes -Take a shorter lunch or break.

Found 10 minutes - Eliminate the things you do each morning to "stall" the starting of your workday.

(You can probably find 20 minutes per day you waste just surfing around on the internet)

You just found thirty minutes per day you can use to make yourself better. Now that doesn't sound like much time, so let me put it in a different perspective. By following these 4 simple suggestions 5 days per week, 50 weeks per year, you just gained 3 forty-hour weeks per year. If you watch TV just 30 minutes less per day, you will double it to 6 forty-hour weeks; that is a lot of extra time to work on "you."

I can think of no better place to put my time than in improving myself. Along with helping myself, it will benefit my family, my company and maybe even rub-off on a few of my friends and associates.

LINE RAISER:
Success has a great deal to do with discipline, so make it a habit to work on "you" just a little bit every day.

What would you say if I had told you I had a guaranteed **"Formula for Success?"** Successful people do what unsuccessful people won't. Successful people don't just arrive at the top of the heap. They had a personal discipline coupled with boundless energy and decided to make things happen. We are all creatures of habit. The problem is, as I have already pointed out, some of those habits could be greatly improved upon. It's your daily habits that will determine your future. Today, I am going to share with you just one short story that could have a profound, positive effect on your future.

> A man approached the late billionaire JP Morgan, held up an envelope and said, *"Sir, in my hand I hold a guaranteed formula for success, which I will gladly sell you for $25,000."* JP Morgan replied, *"Sir, I do not know what is in the envelope, however if you show me, and I like it, I give you my word as a gentleman that I will pay you what you ask."* The man agreed to the terms and handed over the envelope. JP Morgan opened it and took out a single sheet of paper. He gave it one look, just a mere glance, and then handed the single sheet of paper back to the man. JP Morgan then paid the gentleman $25,000. Here is what was written on the paper.
>
> 1. Every morning, write a list of the things that need to be done that day.
>
> 2. Do Them!

Would you pay someone $25,000 for that advice; most people wouldn't, but one of the richest men who had ever lived did. The problem is, by not following the advice, it will cost you a great deal more.

The last book I wrote was entitled *52 Essential Habits for Success,* where I specially and in very concise terms, pointed out the 52 most important habits you should possess if you want to be successful. It never surprises me when I am asked in Q&A sessions after my one of my programs, *"What would be the top 10 habits out of my 52,"* or *"What would be my #1 most important habit to follow?"* So, I will share those two answers with you right now. My Top 10 Habits would be:

> Protect Your Integrity
> Success Requires Self-Discipline
> Believe in Yourself
> Never Give Up
> Never Neglect Your Body

Follow the Golden Rule
Read
Do More Than Expected
Make Goal Setting a Habit
Act as if the Whole World is Watching

If I had to choose just one key factor (habit) that is necessary to be successful it would be DISCIPLINE. There are many other factors involved in becoming successful, such as ... commitment, study, preparation, passion, practice, attitude, persistence, character, and integrity ... but to make it all come together and work, you have to have discipline. Discipline forces you to get up when you don't feel like it, or put in the extra time and effort when everyone else has called it quits. **Discipline is the glue that holds it all together and what separates the good from the great.**

If you want to be a gold medal winner in gymnastics ... it will take a great deal of discipline to train for about eight years, six hours per day. The same is true of all great athletes; they understand without discipline there will be no success. The discipline (practice, time, effort, preparation) required to become a world renowned concert pianist is approximately seventeen years. Great attorneys, doctors, lawyers, Realtors, artists, computer analysts, chefs, teachers, managers, bosses, etc., don't just happen; the greater their discipline, the better they will be.

The matter of achieving greatness and then staying there rests in our ability to maintain discipline. So many great companies have obtained great success only to lose their position of prominence. Lehman Brothers, Arthur Anderson, Circuit City, and Kodak had it all, only to lose their way. Xerox lost 92% of its stock value in two years ... to the tune of $38 billion dollars. Then they chose Anne Mulcahy to try and bring it back. They were $19 billion in debt and their debt-to-equity ratio was 900%. Ms. Mulcahy loved Xerox; she had worked there in sales and human resources for almost 25 years. Most experts believed to save a company this far gone would take a miracle, not a woman who was not even listed in Fortune Magazine's *"50 Most Powerful Women in Business."*

Ms. Mulcahy was exactly what Xerox needed. In 2001 Xerox posted $367 million in losses. In 2006 they posted over $1 billion in profits. She had discipline. She didn't take a weekend off for more than 2 years. She had the discipline to shut-down non-performing business units. She had the discipline to cut $2.5 billion out of their cost structure. She had the discipline not to cut the Research & Development budget; she even increased it.

Discipline is about being able to make the tough decisions, not succumbing to what is popular. Discipline is about being early, doing more than expected, taking nothing for granted, listening to all the facts, getting up every time you get knocked down, and following-up on everything. Discipline is about having a RELENTLESS INTENSITY to get it done. **Don't dwell on the task – dwell on the outcome.** You will find that by looking forward to the outcome it will help to *inspire, create, and produce* an even greater effort.

When things aren't going quite right, when a promotion passes you by, when you didn't get chosen for that special project or you fail at something ... most of the time the fault lies with our own lack of self-discipline. Before you blame others ... look at yourself first.

WHEN YOU COMMIT TO BEING DISCIPLINED YOU CAN PREPARE FOR BEING SUCCESSFUL

DISCIPLINE MAKES ALL LINES RISE

But, before we leave this chapter on habits, I want to share a few more suggestions on things (habits) you should be doing if you plan on being successful.

... SMILE ...
IT'S GOOD FOR YOU
AND THOSE PEOPLE AROUND YOU

To be successful in dealing with people you need to create trust, confidence, and rapport. It is a proven fact that the simple physical response of a smile will help to create all three. If you want to be more successful, have less stress, more friends, and better health, then smile more.

Make it a habit to smile when you answer the phone, shake someone's hand, or greeting anyone. When you are asking someone for help, smile. It's tough to turn down a smile. If you want to change your negative state of mind, smile. People want to be around people who are in good moods and being in a good mood all starts with a smile. Smiling displays your frame of mind and warmth without having to say a word and it puts you in a positive mood; this is all good. Again, it's your choice.

GIVE MORE - GET MORE

Sometimes you can end up getting more by giving more than is necessary. I think the following old story gives a great example of what I mean. *(the author is anonymous)*

> Years ago a city man bought a farm. After taking ownership of his new farm the city man found out the previous owner had been quarreling for years with his neighbor over the location of a fence.
>
> The neighboring farmer immediately tried to quarrel with the new owner, telling him that the fence was a full foot over on his side of the property. The new owner did not get upset, defensive or confrontational with his neighbor. He simply stated, *"Very well, I will set the fence two feet over on my side."*
>
> His surprised neighbor said, *"Oh, but that is more than I claim."* The city man then said, *"Never mind about that. I would much rather have peace with my neighbor than two feet of earth."*
>
> Completely taken back by what the city man had offered to do and his reasoning for doing it, the neighboring farmer replied, *"That's surely fine of you sir, but I couldn't let you do a thing like that."* The fence was never moved.

So many times in life we have the opportunity to diffuse a situation by merely considering the other person's point of view. We should all try to be reasonable and fair in everything we do. But if you throw in a little generosity, you'll find you have fewer problems, leading to less stress and an added bonus; have more friends.

SHOW EXCITEMENT IN YOUR GREETINGS

I have never seen a dog, when its master walks in the door, turn its head and say *"Yo.* **I had a bad day. Not enough water, not enough dog food, you didn't leave the air conditioner on 72°, and the cat has got to go."** A dog is always happy to see its master. The tail is wagging, it's jumping around acting like it hasn't seen its master in months. A dog doesn't do it some of the time, it does it all the time. What a great feeling the dog gives to its master.

The simple expression of *I am really happy to see you* makes anyone feel good. I am not telling you to jump around and look foolish every time you see someone. But I am suggesting you get up, make eye contact, give them a smile and show a genuine interest in them. You will find that people will love to be around you, look forward to seeing you, and include you in their plans, parties and get-togethers. **People love dogs because dogs love people, and they show it. The key words are, "they show it" every time.**

BE NICE

The word "NICE" isn't really a powerful sounding word. On the contrary, it is a simple term used to express a pleasant experience or encounter. I can't really say a person was over-whelmed by what they experienced if they said, *"That was nice." "The meal was nice." "I had a nice time on the date."* Then again, I sure do like it when I encounter a nice person.

I think it is imperative that we put "nice" back into our daily lives both on a professional and personal level. When you look up the word nice in the dictionary you see words like courteous, considerate, friendly, gracious, helpful, kind, polite, and thoughtful when defining the simple word nice. Nice doesn't seem so simple now. How many of us would like to do business with or deal with a courteous, friendly, gracious, helpful, kind, polite, and thoughtful person? No doubt, all of us would.

N.I.C.E. isn't supposed to stand for a **Negative, Irritable, Cranky,** and **Evil** person. The problem today is we seldom encounter NICE anymore. We all seem to be too busy, too rushed, or too pre-occupied to extend a nice pleasantry, kind word, helpful hand, gracious compliment, thoughtful smile, considerate moment to listen, or friendly greeting.

LINE RAISER:

If you want to help put you and/or your business
on the road to success then start incorporating NICE
in to everything you do.
To me, N.I.C.E. is
Necessary, it's Infectious, it's your Choice, and it's Endearing.

You will be amazed how much nicer your day will be when you start being nicer to everyone around you. Let me ask you this: Who would you rather do business with or associate with … a nice person or a negative one? I rest my case.

If you are going through life just in it for you, then you really aren't living, you're just passing through.

CHAPTER 43
How to Deal with Disappointment

Disappointment is inevitable; there are just too many things going on in our lives to not have something or someone disappoint us. There are certainly degrees of disappointments, they come in all sizes, but it's the big ones I want to address today.

People, associates, companies, teachers, bosses, teammates, classmates, spiritual leaders, politicians, spouses, brothers, sisters, Moms and Dads are all on the list of *potential disappointers*. I am writing this because I just had a big disappointment occur. It's not important what happened. What is important is how I will deal with it. Disappointment can lead to frustration, anger, and even bitterness; these are all emotions that will sap the excitement, energy and vitality right out of you. Over the years, I have learned that dwelling on a disappointment won't make it any better, make it go away, or ease the fact that it happened. But occasionally, I still catch myself dwelling on it.

I have no intention of letting anyone or anything keep me down long. That doesn't mean I won't feel the pain, anger, frustration, or hurt at the moment it occurred. But, it does mean I won't keep feeling it. If certain people keep letting you down, then avoid them. The same is true for companies whose product or service fail to meet you expectations; avoid them, too. Thomas Jefferson once said, "*If I am to meet with a disappointment, the sooner I know it, the more of life I shall have to wear it off.*" Disappointments don't just vanish, but as Jefferson noted, they will wear off, if you let it go.

Dwelling on disappointment takes time and energy away from you, which you could be using somewhere else. By dwelling on it, you are actually making it worse. If someone did it on purpose, dwelling on it is allowing them to win even more. I had a football coach once tell me that when I got tackled really hard to *Get-up* off the ground fast, like I was totally unaffected. He said it will rattle your opponent. He said your opponent, who just delivered the painful blow, is thinking they crushed you, hurt you, and beat you. By getting-up fast, as if nothing happened, they will start thinking otherwise. If I can share anything with you today, that will help you better handle disappointment, it would be summed up in having the following reaction;

LINE RAISER:

When a disappointment knocks you down …
Get up fast! Get over it! Let it go! Move on!

I heard it once stated, *"Disappointment to a noble soul is what cold water is to burning metal; it strengthens, tempers, intensifies, but never destroys it."* What an incredible way to look at it. The key words there are, *Noble Soul.*

The level of success in your life comes from the choices you make.
When it comes to dealing with disappointment, be the Noble Soul and MOVE ON!

Admiral Robert Peary had a dream. He was committed to be the first to find the exact location of the North Pole and be the first to stand upon it; the first to stand on top of the world. He had failed seven times trying to reach the North Pole. Seven hundred fifty-six other men before him had attempted the quest only to lose their lives. Admiral Peary had encountered enormous hardships, broken bones and lost several toes to frostbite in his attempts, but at least he was still alive.

On April 6, 1909, on his eighth attempt, he finally reached his goal. At his gravesite in Arlington National Cemetery you will find written on his tombstone his personal credo:

Inveniam viam aut facium,
"I shall find a way or make one."

I once heard the statement that the difference between a "Big Shot" and a "Little Shot" was that *the "Big Shot" was a "Little Shot" who just kept on shooting.* You might consider the statement corny, but it's true. Right now things might not look so bright for you. You may have been passed over for a promotion, had a terrible sales year, lost money in a business deal or the stock market, been fired, feeling old / tired / out-of-shape, or just seem to be in a really bad rut. You may be wondering how you are ever going to possibly turn things around.

The first thing to understand is that many extremely successful people have lost their direction, made wrong decisions or just failed miserably. The difference is that their failure was for the moment. To them, it was just a setback. There is an old Japanese proverb for success: *"Fall seven times, stand up eight."* The only person you need to believe in you, IS YOU. Ted Turner, Donald Trump, Walt Disney, Winston Churchill, Albert Einstein, Oprah Winfrey, and Christopher Reeve, to name just a few, all overcame some major setback in their lives. There is nothing you can do about your past; what is done is done. It is what you are going to do now that counts.

LINE RAISER:
Failure is just an experience that didn't work out.
Learn from it, reorganize, re-energize, redefine your focus,
redirect your efforts, and move on.

In other words …

Find A Way or Make One … But Keep Moving On!

CHAPTER 44
Do You Annoy People

Do you annoy people? Do you have a certain habit that really bothers the heck out of family, friends, and associates? I have one relative who blows their nose at the dinner table every time they come over. Right in the middle of eating, out comes the handkerchief, and BAM, you know what's coming next. Every Thanksgiving, Christmas, Easter, birthdays, no matter what the occasion, you can count on **the big blow.**

There are people who follow almost every sentence with the phrase, *"you know"* or *"you know what I mean."* You might know that person who uses the term *"like"* in almost every sentence; *"Like, you know what I mean ... Like, they really bother me ... Like, get over it."* Do you smack your food when you eat? I'm not real fond of the person who chew their gum so you get to see it quite often. The list can go on and on; talking loud on your cell-phone, wearing too much cologne or perfume, twirling your hair, biting your nails, or always late.

I had a terrible habit of always stealing the punch line when my wife was telling a funny story. One day she finally said, *"Do you always have to interrupt me and tell the ending."* I remember saying, *"But I thought you had finished."* Her reply was, *"No, I just took a breath."* I hadn't realized that I was doing it. I just got wrapped up in her story and was helping her finish. Now that's annoying.

Having children may also help to have your annoying habits identified. One day my son said, *"Hey Dad, you enjoying those peanuts?"* I said, *"Yeah, why do you ask?"* He said, *"Because I can hear you eating them all the way over here."* I can't stand people who eat loud ... but there I was ... eating loud.

Being a professional speaker there are many times my program is videotaped. Each one of those tapes is a great learning experience for me when I review them. Tapes don't lie; they show you everything you are doing right and everything you may be doing wrong. The audience might not pick up on it, but I do. In fact, if I catch myself over-using a particular phrase, I will write that phrase out in large print on a 3 X 5 card and place it close by me when I speak for the next several weeks, to remind myself to not over-use that phrase.

It is most likely that you won't be videotaping yourself to help catch you doing those annoying things. You may not have that teenager who will help you change your ways. But, it might behoove you to ask a few close friends or relatives if you do have any annoying habits. Don't take umbrage with what they say. Remember, you asked. Now, you may think you don't have any annoying habits … and my response to you would be … *think again!*

If people are annoying you, I have but one word for you: **CHILL!** Years ago, my son Tyler and I were driving around running a few errands and to our misfortune we encounter a jerk. Now jerks can come in all shapes, sizes, ages, genders, and calibers. I use the word caliber in context to the degree of jerk they are; inconsiderate jerk, pestering jerk, annoying jerk, or off-the-chart jerk. The one we encountered was an off-the-chart jerk!

I popped off in the car to Tyler about what a jerk this man was, yada, yada, yada, and Tyler can hear and see that I am noticeably angered by the situation. He looks at me and says, **"Dad, CHILL!"** Now if I had ever said that to my father, you probably wouldn't be reading this today. Tyler and I have a different kind of relationship. He wasn't being a flippant teenager with a smart mouth. He was actually concerned about my health.

He went on to put the matter in a very proper perspective. He said, ***"Dad, in the last seven months we have moved out-of-state into a rental home, then moved into a home we purchased in that state, then moved back to Florida. What this man is doing that bothers you is nothing compared to what we have been through."*** You know what, he was right. I was wound a little too tight from all that we had been through and was letting something trivial get to me. I decided to do something with Tyler's so appropriate word **CHILL,** and make an acronym for the word as a reminder of his excellent advice:

C. H. I. L. L.
Calm Helps Individuals Live Longer

> # LINE RAISER:
> So, the next time you get angered, annoyed, or frustrated about something, just remember to CHILL.
> It will be better for your health, your attitude and especially those around you who are witnessing your angered state.
>
> # ANGER never raises any line.

Southwest Airlines strives to hire people with a sense of humor. They found that if you have a sense of humor you thrive during change, remain creative under pressure, work more effectively, play more enthusiastically, and stay healthier in the process. Companies have also found that people with a sense of humor are accepted better by their peers and customers; in other words, people with a sense of humor are less ANNOYING than those without one. The CEO of Starbucks once was quoted as saying, *"We hire for smiles and we promote for smiles."*

What if you were looking for a job and in your interview they handed you the following list and asked you to put a check mark by the characteristics which best suit you; which ones would you leave blank? *(I realize some of these are similar ... but just go with me on this.)*

__Knowledgeable	__Enthusiastic	__Energetic
__Happy	__Prompt	__Dedicated
__Accommodating	__Resourceful	__Upbeat
__Caring	__Attentive	__Gracious
__Well-Mannered	__Professional	__Pleasant
__Friendly	__Focused	__Polite
__Sense-of-humor	__Approachable	__Efficient
__Kind	__Helpful	__Fast
__Go-Getter	__Observant	__Realistic
__Tactful	__Truthful	__Likeable

I hope you noticed I didn't have ANNOYING on the list.
That is one trait employers, customers and associates can do without.

To me, success in life and business is all about learning how to get better, and then using that knowledge to improve. A lot of times having a personal scorecard or a way to rate yourself can really help identify where you might need some help. Let's go back to the list for a moment and look at some of the characteristics you didn't check. If you didn't check HAPPY does that mean you are sad, depressed, moody, grumpy, glum, irritable or what? If you didn't check PROMPT does that mean you are always late? If you aren't TACTFUL, then I guess you must be rude.

Just look at the implications of what the opposite of these words mean. If you aren't GRACIOUS does that mean you might be nasty, mean, sarcastic or hateful? If you didn't check ENERGETIC, does that mean you are lazy or slow? By looking at the opposite of what each word means, this list starts to take on a whole new perspective. The answers to "which ones are you" now become very profound.

My challenge to you is … why not be all of them? That doesn't mean that you are going to be all of these things … ALL OF THE TIME. But, you do need to recognize the value of them and always strive to be identified as a person who has these powerful characteristics. I had a person one time ask me, *"Rob, are you always in a good mood?"* My response was, *"No, but I am always trying to get there."*

Now, go back and take another look at your list of checked characteristics and ask yourself, would my five closest friends, my boss and three business associates REALLY agree with me? If you feel strongly that they would agree, then keep it checked. If not, then start working on making it so they would agree.

LINE RAISER:
**The first step to improving is identifying your faults,
especially your annoying ones.
Your *Line Starts Rising*
when you start correcting them.**

CHAPTER 45
Being Scared Helps You Get Through

Sometimes life throws you a curveball and introduces a trauma or an unexpected event that will forever change your life. I'd like to take you back to May 22, 2000; on that day the life of my son, wife and I would never be the same. Six words were spoken to us, just six words that **scared us to death;**

"Your son has type 1 diabetes."

The moment those words were spoken, everything changed. At first, as a nine-year-old, our son Tyler had no idea what had just happened. Being told that there was no Santa Claus was a whole lot more traumatic than being told he had diabetes. We were thrust into a battle to make sure our son would be okay ... and **we were scared.** We read books and went online to watch videos to gain as much information as we could to help him ... and **we were still scared.**

There were days when his blood sugar levels were off so badly that we had to test his blood over twenty times ... **and we were scared.** At one point, Tyler was taking as many as ten shots per day and his fingers became pincushions with the constant pricking to draw blood to test his glucose levels. His doctor then put Tyler on an insulin pump ... and that pump **scared us even more.** Would the pump fail, would it give him too much insulin, would he go into diabetic shock ... all those thoughts and many more ran through our brain.

We have learned a lot since that diagnosis. We found that **being scared** allowed our body to pull together all its energy and resourcefulness to help us get through it. His doctor showed us that Tyler could accomplish anything he wanted as long as we helped him stay vigilant in controlling his blood sugar levels. We even consider ourselves fortunate because he had a disease that can be controlled.

Tyler wrote, in his essay to be considered for college, the following excerpt.

"I think that the discipline I have learned in controlling my diabetes will be a major factor in helping me succeed

in life. Helen Keller said, 'Face your deficiencies and acknowledge them, but do not let them master you.' I understand that I can never relax from being disciplined, and that is okay: It is what it is. Being upset that I have diabetes will do nothing to help me deal with it. I feel lucky that I have a disease that can be controlled. You can't always control the challenges that you will face in life, but you can control how you will deal with them. Diabetes has shown me the importance of discipline, vigilance, and determination if we are to overcome the difficulties and deficiencies that we encounter in life."

I shared this story with you because many of you out there, right now, are going through some kind of trauma or ordeal and **you're scared.** Well, that's okay. It's a natural reaction and a helpful stimulus to keep you sharp and give you the strength to deal with it; the key words are ... DEAL WITH IT. Our son's situation has taught us you can get through it; our **being scared** has now turned into being extremely focused. Tyler is doing great and so will you.

LINE RAISER:

If you want to Raise Your Line,
just remember Ms. Keller's words ...

*"Face your deficiencies
and
acknowledge them,
but do not let them master you."*

CHAPTER 46
Get Over It and Move On

Sometimes, you get bad advice. Sometimes, you make a wrong decision because of bad advice. Sometimes, you don't realize what you are doing isn't going to work. Sometimes, you have no idea that what you are doing is going to make you look silly or unprofessional. Sometimes, what you think might be a great idea, turns out to be just the opposite. Sometimes, you get lucky, and someone else looks past all of those "sometimes" and still gives you a chance.

When I decided to become a professional speaker I sought the advice of several people and even flew out to the National Speakers Association's Annual conference and walked around for two days, listening, reading and questioning anyone who would talk to me. It seemed to me from all the advice I was getting, I had to have something that would get me noticed, set me apart and differentiate me from all the other speakers ... be it a gimmick, a nickname, some approach that would make me intriguing, memorable and make them want to hire Robert Stevenson. A friend of mine recommended I use my nickname, *"Robin Hood."* We don't have enough time to go into how I got the nickname today, but it was memorable. Maybe it would cause some intrigue, enough to make an agent want to call.

(Remember, this was back in the days before we emailed everything – the client was actually going to be receiving something in the mail)

Oh, I went at the **Robin Hood** idea in a big way. We're talking green ink *(Sherwood Forest Green)* and parchment paper for the brochure. I even found an old drawing of **Robin Hood** that I put on the front cover. To hold all the pages together in my incredibly professional media package (or so I thought), I had a green plastic spiral to match the green ink.

But wait, it gets worse. My **Robin Hood** drawing showed him wearing a hat that had one feather in it. So, with another stroke of brilliance, I decided to buy a bunch of small white feathers and place one feather in each media packet, so when it was opened, the feather would gently float out of the envelope and fall to their desk. You can't make this stuff up – I really did all of this.

But, I wasn't finished. Oh no, I even went further into the abyss, by having the following Closing Line; *"Hiring Robert Stevenson will put a feather in your cap!"* ... assuming they would know sticking a feather in their cap was a sign of achievement or success. Then I sent this, memorable, thought-provoking, attention getting disaster out to over 50 of the top booking agencies in the United States. Surprise, surprise, I didn't get one call. Not only did I not get one call, I couldn't get anyone to take my calls or return the messages I left. It was a total bust until finally, Lois Brown, a cagey veteran agent who owned a booking agency in Tampa, Florida, took my call.

Lois said that she had been looking forward to meeting the person who had the guts to send such a package. She said she wanted to thank me for giving her one of the best and longest laughs she had had in years. Then, I'll never forget her next words. Lois said, *"Rob, I actually got past your marketing catastrophe and read your bio and I think you can make it in this industry."* She said she would start booking me, only if I would NEVER bring up Robin Hood again. Lois also said she was not interested in gimmicks, only content and delivery.

When somebody new, young, or unfamiliar with your business throws out an idea or thought, that at first blush, you think is NUTS ... try looking for what might be right with the idea ... not what is wrong with it. Jack Welch, former CEO of GE, once said – *"The Hero is the one with ideas."* Not all ideas are great, I get that. But, the more ideas you throw out there, the better chance you have to succeed.

In 1985, Coca-Cola changed its formula and brought out New Coke. It was a marketing disaster, it made them the laughing stock of the industry, consumers were furious *(over 400,000 calls and letters complaining)*, it cost them tons of money, and they went back to their original formula three months later. But, because it brought so much attention to Classic Coke, six months later Classic Coke sales were increasing at double the rate of Pepsi.

Yes, my first idea stunk ... but I'm still a professional speaker twenty-four years later. I learned from it, adjusted my tactics and moved on. My **Robin Hood** Media Packet is in a file cabinet and I refer to it from time to time, reminding myself from wince I came. Success is not about where you start, it is about where you finish.

Be Bold – Do Something New - Go Stick a Feather in YOUR Cap

To me a real mistake/failure is due to a lack of knowledge or skill. I will not let it define who I am or stop me. I will learn from it and MOVE ON. A misstep, as the story I just told you, is also not going to define who I am. So you blew it, you messed up, you lost, you missed, you made a mistake, blunder, gaffe, got it wrong, or slipped-up ... well, welcome to the human race. I am so tired of people saying, *"I woulda, I shoulda, I coulda,"* or talking about regrets and old mistakes. If you plan on being successful, you will need to learn how to GET OVER IT and MOVE ON when things don't go as planned.

To me, a road block is just a detour, a defeat is only a set-back, and a *"so-called"* failure is a learning experience. While researching for his book **Think and Grow Rich**, the great writer Napoleon Hill discovered that, in most cases for over 500 millionaires he interviewed, *success came "after" their greatest failure.* Albert Einstein said, *"Anyone who has never made a mistake has never tried anything new."* Regardless of the strategy we employ in our quest to succeed, we will have both successes and failures; usually a whole lot more failures than success.

Let me remind you again, Abraham Lincoln went to war a captain and returned a private. He also failed as a businessman and a lawyer, had a nervous breakdown, turned to politics and was defeated seven times before being elected President. He once wrote in a letter to a friend saying, *"I am now the most miserable man living."*

Tom Watson, Sr., the founder of IBM, was being interviewed by a young man who asked the following question. *"Mr. Watson, how can I be great like you?"* Without any hesitation Mr. Watson responded, *"Double your failures."* As long as you are learning from your mistakes and applying that knowledge so you can proceed more intelligently the next time, you win. Just think how British fiction writer John Creasey must have felt getting 774 rejection notices before selling his first story; now that is a persistent, tenacious, determined, committed man. He went on to write over 600 novels using 28 different pseudonyms. The first book that started the *Chicken Soup for the Soul* franchise was rejected 134 times before selling over 1 million copies. Remember, **failure is only failure when you quit trying.**

There are so many ways I have heard it stated: *Fail Forward Fast, Failures are Stepping Stones to Success, Failure is the Ultimate Teacher, and Fail Intelligently,* are just a few of the words of wisdom for us to follow. Here are a few more ways to look at failure from some rather reputable people.

Failure is only the opportunity to begin again more intelligently.
Henry Ford

Success is going from failure to failure without losing your enthusiasm.
Abraham Lincoln

Failure doesn't mean you are a failure... it just means you haven't succeeded yet.
Robert Schuller

Never confuse a single defeat with a final defeat.
F. Scott Fitzgerald

LINE RAISER:
Life isn't easy, learning isn't simple,
errors, mistakes, and losing aren't fun ....
Never forget that failure is a major component
of the learning process, so ...
GET OVER IT and MOVE ON.

Sometimes it's good to reflect from whence we came to appreciate how good we have it now. If you are new at what you are doing, you might ask some folks who have been at your company for a long time to share some of their growing pain stories. Yes, reflection is good and sometimes leads to some incredible stories and a whole lot of laughter. So, to get things started, I thought you might enjoy one of my reflections.

I had just gotten into the speaking business when I received a call from a friend of a friend who had heard about me and the next thing you know ... I'm booked to speak to about 500 people in a convention hall in central Florida. I was fired up. It was mid-July, but the AC was working in both my car and in the convention center, so heat and humidity shouldn't be an issue. I had inquired when I arrived where the restrooms were, because I always make a "pit-stop" before I speak. They served dinner first and I was sitting at the head table at the far left end.

About 10 minutes before I was to speak, I slipped out from the table unnoticed to make my "pit-stop" before giving my speech. I went to a double door that you push open with a big bar in the middle and entered a dark hall. *(This, I found out later, was not the door they had been pointing to when I received my directions to the restrooms.)* I kept walking for a ways and had to go through another door, with more additional walking, until I found a restroom. Little did I know that the second door I went through locked behind me. There was no way to get back the way I came and no one could hear my banging or yelling ... nor had they seen me slip out.

In my mind, I had one alternative and that was to climb out the bathroom window and walk around the building. It was a long drop out the window, so there was no getting back in ... but at least I was outside. I didn't realize I was dropping into an eight foot high chain-linked fenced-in area behind the convention center. I now had to climb the fence to be able to walk around the building. You have got to picture this ... here I was in a great looking suit, perfectly manicured to present my program before going to the restroom ... now, I was sweating bullets, destroying my suit, getting filthy, and to top it off, I was wearing a blue shirt that is showing just how bad I was sweating. *(Never wear a blue shirt in the summer.)*

I threw my suit coat over the fence, climbed over, and I'm finally free. I walked all the way around the convention center and up to the front door and entered the hall. The man who had hired me was at the podium making small talk ... wondering where in the world I had gone, when he looked up and said ... *"Well, here he is now, Mr. Robert Stevenson."* He pointed towards the back of the convention hall and there I stood in all my glory. The gasps and whispers were abundant as I made my way to the front.

There is an old Chinese saying, *"When the tiger enters the temple, make it part of the ceremony,"* and that is exactly what I did. I couldn't hide what had happened, so I made it part of my program. I told the audience the complete story and they were howling with laughter. Somebody handed me several cloth napkins to wipe off and then I started. The audience was with me from the get-go and, I hope to this day, they still are.

It has been over 24 years and 2,500 speeches later, but one of the proudest moments of my speaking career was making it to the front of that hall and facing that audience.

Sometimes things aren't going to go as planned. Sometimes you are going to stumble, bumble, or fall, and that's okay; it happens to the best. But what makes them the best is they got up and carried on. Do yourself a favor and reflect on life's lessons and smile; you made it, you survived, and you will survive the next time.

LINE RAISER:
Intelligence is realizing mistakes will happen,
so learn from them and move on.
Wisdom is understanding those
missteps, mistakes and blunders
are the foundation for your success.

Even brilliant people royally mess up. John Joseph Merlin was a very successful maker of clocks and precision instruments. He also designed weighing machines and wheelchairs, improved musical instruments, and even spent much of his time trying to develop a perpetual motion machine. This highly intelligent man was also a talented musician who enjoyed playing both the harpsichord and violin. With this background, you might find it surprising that he is remembered for the man who invented the "Roller-Skate."

In 1760, he convinced himself that he could travel faster by foot if he would just strap wheels to his shoes. When was the last time you sat in a meeting where someone came up with an idea, and your first thought was, that will never work? But, let's say you are an open-minded person, and give them the latitude to prove their ridiculous idea. Would you still think the idea had potential if it failed miserably when they first demonstrated it?

Let's go back to 1760 where John Merlin had been working on increasing the speed and efficiency of walking. He attached two wheels to a metal plate and then strapped them to his shoes (the first in-line skates) and after countless attempts to stand and skate ... IT WORKED! Having been invited to a huge social event, a masked ball at the Carlisle House in the upscale SoHo Square district of London, Mr. Merlin decided to unveil his new invention there. He didn't play it safe. John decided to enter the grand ballroom on his roller skates while playing his violin; this was going to be a glorious moment for him. In front of the elite socialites of London, John skated in and lost his balance, crashed into a massive expensive mirror, destroying the mirror, his violin, and his pride.

Had you been a witness of this enormous failure, would you immediately discount the idea as stupid, silly, ridiculous ... or would you look at the concept and think there might be some potential? Did Mr. Merlin fail because it was a stupid idea or did he fail because he was not a very skilled skater who increased his chances for failure by playing his violin while skating? Had he not been playing a violin, could he have used his hands to possibly correct his balance as he headed for the mirror, thus making his grand entrance a success?

Mr. Merlin's "SPECTACULAR" failure set back the use of roller-skates for several decades. It takes a special person to see past failure and look for potential. It takes a special person to keep working at an idea to finally make it succeed. It takes a very special person to see every failure as a learning experience ... as what not to do ... and keep trying to find what should be done.

LINE RAISER:
Never forget that success comes to those
who see past failure,
so always look for potential and realize
not all great ideas worked the first time.

CHAPTER 47
"That's Not My Job"

I find many people fail to advance within a company because they don't take responsibility for the overall success of the company. It is as if they perform their job with blinders on; ignoring anything that is going on around them. They have decided that they are ONLY responsible for their job, function, task, assignment, or duty, and nothing else. Now, I am not suggesting that you should mettle in other people's jobs. But, when you see a problem or mistake getting ready to happen that could be avoided if you just took a moment to bring it to their attention, I think you should speak up; especially if it is going to cost the company money or the loss of a customer.

Years ago, I came across a wonderful explanation of what I am suggesting. I think when you read it you will better understand the point I am trying to make.

This is a story about four people named,
Everybody, Somebody, Anybody,* and *Nobody.
There was an important job to be done,
and *Everybody* was sure that *Somebody* would do it.
***Anybody* could have done it, but *Nobody* did.**
***Somebody* got angry about that,**
because it was *Everybody's* job.
***Everybody* thought *Anybody* could do it,**
but *Nobody* realized that *Everybody* wouldn't do it.
It ended up that *Everybody* blamed *Somebody*
when *Nobody* did what *Anybody* could have.

(Author Unknown)

I know successful companies are looking for people who are willing to **take the initiative**; people willing to do something even if they haven't been asked to do it. If you want to advance in your company, I suggest that when you see a problem, take the initiative to fix it without waiting for a directive to come down from your boss. You can focus on just your job or you can also be concerned about helping to make your company be successful. Personally, if I was putting together a team of people for a major project, I want people who are both FOCUSED and CONCERNED.

It is as simple as oiling a door that has squeaky hinges. Every time *Somebody* opens that door it makes an annoying, squeaky noise that bothers *Everybody* in the room. *Anybody* could have taken the initiative to oil the hinges, but *Nobody* did. *Everybody* thought *Somebody* would eventually oil the hinges ... but you guessed it ... *Nobody* did it. If you were working for me and I found that your "REAL" attitude was ...*that is not my job, I wasn't hired to do that, or that is beneath my job title* ... you soon wouldn't be working for me. Start being the *Somebody* who does what *Anybody* could have done, but *Nobody* took the initiative to do. Because if you do, *Everybody* is going to want you on their team.

What Do Initiative and Success Have In Common?
Everything!

LINE RAISER:
Never say ...
"That's not my job!"

Mark Twain said, *"Thunder is good, thunder is impressive; but it is lightning that does the work."* Don't impress me with your words, impress me with your deeds *(your lightning).* If you want to differentiate yourself, your company, or organization from your competition, then set out to impress people with the job you do ... every time!

I have a list of people I can call on, who are experts at what they do. But, the reason I call upon them is that they always ***IMPRESS ME*** with their finished product or service; they give me splendid, superb, and well-done ... ***EVERY TIME.***

There are a lot of people and companies out there who talk a great story, but they never seem to deliver on what they promised.

"Now that was impressive."
"They did an impressive job."
"I must say, I was impressed."
"I had my doubts, but the finished result is impressive."

Statements like those are what lead you to success. To have people **impressed** with your ***work effort, or diligence, or thoroughness, or focus, or attention to the details, or creativity, or innovative ideas, or persistence,*** will keep people wanting to do business with you and keep you employed.

There is an old proverb which states: ***"If a job is worth doing, it's worth doing well."*** On October 26, 1967, six months before Dr. Martin Luther King, Jr. was assassinated, he spoke to students at Barratt Junior High School in Philadelphia. His message was based on the premise that regardless of your position in life, you should always **strive to be the best** at what you do. He used the example of a street sweeper to make his point. Dr. King stated;

"If a man is called to be a street sweeper,
he should sweep streets even as Michelangelo painted,
or Beethoven composed music, or Shakespeare wrote poetry.
He should sweep streets so well that
all the hosts of heaven and earth will pause to say,
'Here lived a great street sweeper who did his job well.'"

Impress me with your knowledge, enthusiasm, professionalism, energy, efficiency, upbeat attitude, along with your caring, accommodating, helpful manner, and I will forever want to keep doing business with you.

LINE RAISER:

In Every Job You Do Show It Your Full Respect
by Always Giving Your Very Best
Seek to Impress – Every Time

CHAPTER 48
There is No Success Without Ex's

I was invited to speak at FedEx World Headquarters where I delivered two programs. I also had the wonderful opportunity to take a tour of their Memphis Hub Operations and see how they are able to process over 600,000 packages per night while it was actually happening. It was an amazing sight to behold.

I wanted to talk to them on a personal level so they could advance their own careers, while at the same time helping their company. I also wanted to create something special for those who attended my sessions that would be memorable and have a direct correlation with FedEx. Then it hit me ... the "Ex" in their corporate name ... stands for so much more than "Express." Just as FedEx has added, evolved, changed, tweaked, and greatly improved on everything they do, I told my audience they, too, needed to do the same. I then gave them a list of "Ex's" to follow that would ensure not only their success in business, but also in life. I told them they needed to ask themselves:

Do I Excel at my job?

Do I always give Extra?

Do I Exert maximum effort?

Do I avoid making Excuses?

Do I set the right Examples?

Do I Exceed what is required?

Do I Exhibit the best judgment?

Do I always strive for Excellence?

Do I Exemplify the best standards?

Do I Exhaust all possible solutions?

Do I always Extend a helping hand?

Do I strive to be Exceptional at my job?

Do I Experiment at new ways to do things?

Do I Execute according to proper procedures?

Do my peers considered me an Expert at what I do?

Do I Examine all mistakes to fully understand their cause?

Regardless what company, association, or organization you work for, if you follow this list of "Ex's," everyone will want you. You will be known as the person they can always count on because you always deliver ... you will be **Exceptional.**

To establish and maintain a position of supremacy in anything you do requires that you start incorporating the "Ex's" in all aspects of your life and business. It's your choice ... you can either do it or you will simply be "Excluded" from that list of people who succeed in life and that is the one "Ex" I surely want to stay away from. So remember...

LINE RAISER:

Let the "Ex's" mark your path
on your journey towards success.

Successful people have a lot of different talents, skills, and abilities, along with some interesting attributes, qualities, and characteristics, but they don't all have the same ones. Personally, I like successful people who are humble, caring, kind, and pleasant. I think there is more to being successful than just rank or money. But, I have found that there isn't just one path, one set way, one magic formula, one way of acting, that will lead you down the path to being successful.

In my over twenty years of researching successful people, a trait I found they all seem to have in common with each other is the attitude of **"I Got This."** They have the confidence to jump in and make things happen, the energy to see it through, and the willpower to stick with it until it is done. When people bring them a problem, need, request, or plea for help, they all seem to move into another gear ... the **"I Got This"** gear.

Having an **"I Got This"** attitude is not for everyone. It requires giving **EXTRA** as though it's a matter of course. It requires energy and stamina with a morale boosting spirit. If you are wondering if you are "that" person in your organization or headed in that direction

… all you need to do is count up how many times people are requesting your help. If you find that you are being called on a lot by your peers and bosses, then it looks like you are headed in the right direction. BUT, if you find that people seem to leave you alone, then you might have a problem. The easier your job becomes and the less involved you seem to be, the simpler it is to replace you. A person who can be counted on to deliver in any situation is invaluable to any organization.

Laziness is a deadly disease that destroys careers.

To me, there is another way to think about the Ex's, such as: always giving EXtra, always EXceeding what is required, always EXhausting all possibilities … is to simply do MORE: **the most effective tool for success is the "MORE" Tool**

I find companies and people achieve MORE when they give MORE. Sometimes the simplest gesture can make a great impact on your customer. Try to figure out what might really impress your customer that is above and beyond what you (and your competition) normally do. Here are some examples:

▶ They offer to carry your bags to your car
▶ They shipped your merchandise free
▶ They honor the sale price from yesterday's ad
▶ They know more about their merchandise than their competitors
▶ They seem genuinely happy to service your every need
▶ You get a free dessert because they took too long on your order
▶ Your glass is never empty because the waiter is always there to fill it up
▶ Service personnel put on shoe "booties" before entering your home
▶ You take your car in for an oil change - they also vacuum your car and clean your windshield

When you create a culture where everyone in your company is striving to do MORE than expected you will be amazed at the results. Your greatest form of advertising is word-of-mouth. Angie's List has become a huge success by being a great word-of-mouth network that helps over 1 million members find the best service. U.S. News & World Report wrote: *"Angie's List is an invaluable repository of informed judgments on an increasing deep inventory of service providers."* A great way for you to see how consumers define what "MORE" really is would be to check out Angie's List.

The same is true for you personally. The most effective tool for success is the "MORE" tool.

LINE RAISER:

▶ **Do more than you should**
▶ **Study more than is necessary**
▶ **Practice more than is expected**
▶ **Prepare more than you have to**
▶ **Deliver more than they imagined**
▶ **Be more cheerful, courteous and compassionate to others**

And your success will be far "MORE" than you ever expected.

Just because you are giving your all, doing the extra things, and delivering more than expected, that doesn't mean obtaining success is immediately going to happen. But, if you read on a little further, I will show you how you can **Go Anywhere You Want To Go.**

She was newly divorced, living on welfare, caring for a small child, and having to live with her sister and brother-in-law because she couldn't afford a place of her own. She wrote a book in long hand, retyped it on a manual typewriter, and then snuck into a computer lounge of a local college and retyped it on a computer, terrified that she would be discovered as a nonstudent. After a year of rejections from publishers, Bloomsbury bought Harry Potter and the Philosopher's Stone (Philosopher was changed to Sorcerer for the US market) and the rest is history. Now, after selling over 400 million books and having several successful movies based on those books, J.K. Rowling is one of the richest women in the world.

I can give you example after example of people who OVERCAME incredible odds to finally make it. Go check out the stories of Rachel Ray, Shania Twain, Winston Churchill, Dr. Phil McGraw, Kurt Warner, Ted Turner, and Mary Kay Ash. You will be amazed what these people overcame to become successful.

Sometimes things don't work out according to our own time table or expectations. World famous author, Theodor Seuss Geisel *(you would know him best as Dr. Seuss)*, who has sold over one hundred million copies of his books, was no overnight success. In fact, forty-three publishers rejected his first book until a friend published it. There were no great accolades, incredible reviews, or any fanfare made over the book; it did okay. It wasn't until seventeen years later that his career took off because he filled a need.

The magazine publishing giant Life Magazine had published a report that schoolchildren were having difficulty learning how to read because all the books they were reading were boring. Dr. Seuss's publisher friend challenged him to write a kids book with less than 250 words that wouldn't be boring; that challenge produced **The Cat in the Hat.** It took him seventeen years from writing a mediocre book to becoming world famous.

Life is full of setbacks, bad surprises,
unwanted obstacles, and unfair difficulties.
I have heard it countless times, "Life Sucks."
Well, just because life sucks sometimes,
doesn't mean you need to let it suck the life out of you.

Dr. Seuss was a seventeen year OVERNIGHT success; there is nothing wrong with that. Sure we would all like it to happen immediately, but that usually isn't the case. **If you knew that by hanging-in-there just a little longer you would be successful ... then you would stay the course?**

When things get tough, remind yourself that Ms. Rowling went from welfare to billionaire. Just as books have many chapters, so does your life. The beauty about writing a book and living your life is you get to make the decisions as to how you want them both to turn out.

Persistence and Courage Can Take You Anywhere You Want To Go,

so decide today where it is you want to go and let your journey begin.

To paraphrase Calvin Coolidge:

"Nothing in the world can take the place of

Persistence.

'Press On' has solved and always will solve the problems of the human race."

LINE RAISER:
Regardless of the circumstances or outcome, you must always ... PRESS ON!

CHAPTER 49
Mistaken for the Maître D'

Several years ago I had the opportunity to be the after dinner keynote speaker for a major insurance company. It was an awards dinner honoring their top producers both nationally and internationally. It was quite a fancy affair with beautiful table arrangements, dim lighting, and everyone all dressed up.

All the foreign award winners were in the back of the room where headsets had been provided, along with interpreters so they could listen to my program in their native language. I always like to stand at the back of the room before I speak to get a full view of what my audience sees, mapping out where I should and shouldn't stand during my presentation. So, there I was about 15 minutes before going on, standing against the back wall in the dimly lit room, deep in thought. My thoughts were interrupted abruptly with the loud snapping of fingers by a Japanese gentleman waving at me. I walked over to him, and in broken English, he said, ***"We need more chairs here for ladies."*** I guess he thought I was the Maître d' because I was standing there overlooking what was going on.

So, I said, ***"No problem,"*** and went and got some chairs. I took my position back up against the wall waiting to be introduced, when the finger snapping and waving happened again by the same man. I walked over and said, ***"Do you need more chairs?"*** … to which he responded, ***"Yes."*** I gathered up a few more chairs while keeping an eye on the podium, because I was now being introduced, and needed to start inconspicuously easing up to the front of the room. I delivered the chairs and told the gentleman I had to go now. There was a puzzled look on his face, as if he wasn't through with me yet … but I didn't have time to explain. I made a respectful bow to the gentleman and proceeded to the front of the room.

After my program was over a group of Japanese people were following ***"my finger snapper"*** and were all heading my way. He stopped in front of me and gave a deep bow while at the same time apologizing for his actions. Words like ***"please forgive"*** … ***"I had no idea you speaker"*** … ***"I so sorry"*** … were flowing out of his mouth. I guess he thought he had insulted me by asking me to get the chairs. *(The way I was raised – if ladies need chairs you go get them chairs – there was no insult.)* I bowed politely and with a big grin on my face said, **"You have nothing to apologize for - the ladies needed chairs and I was happy to oblige."**

After several more moments of conversation I was able to get him to relax and even smile; there was no harm, no foul, or disgrace. The only disgrace that could have occurred is if I didn't get the chairs. I was taught to treat all people with respect. Position, status, or lack-there-of should have nothing to do with the way we treat anyone. But, I see people disrespecting peers, associates, or subordinates all the time. I see managers talking down to those reporting to them as if they are some big "Muckity Muck" who should be feared and revered. If your attitude is perceived that a certain task is beneath you, management is not the place for you.

Respect is an earned title … not a given one. I find it very unappealing and unnecessary to talk down to anyone. A better-than-thou attitude can hurt you far more than it can, if ever, help you. Those who revere STATUS more than RESPECT will NEVER excel as true LEADERS.

LINE RAISER:
Always show respect to others regardless of their status. Respecting others can never hurt you – disrespect can.

CHAPTER 50
TCS Training

For several years I have been involved in an extensive training program called TCS Training. This program has helped me immensely in both my personal and business development. Many of the things that were presented to me I already knew, obvious points of information, but were important enough to be addressed again and again. I would like to share a few of these points with you so you, too, can gain from the knowledge of my instructor.

- ➢ Saying *"Thank You"* is powerful.
- ➢ Having a great imagination is important, and so is having fun.
- ➢ Persistence will usually get you what you want.
- ➢ The more you read the more you learn.
- ➢ Being excited to see someone makes that someone feel special.
- ➢ Failure is a major component of the learning process.
- ➢ People are going to disappoint you and not mean to.
- ➢ Being FORGIVING is a trait you MUST possess.
- ➢ Your way is not necessarily the only way to get something done.
- ➢ It's amazing what people will do for a prize, or just a little praise.
- ➢ Practice makes things easier to do and showing is more effective than telling.
- ➢ Laughter is infectious, good for you, and good for those around you, so pass it on.
- ➢ Sometimes you have to tell people more than once what you expect of them.
- ➢ *"No"* really doesn't mean no, it just means you need to take a different approach.
- ➢ It is more effective to get people to WANT TO do something than HAVE TO.

Now, I realize that most of these points aren't profound. For many of us, we have heard them time and time again. But, what might make them a little more surprising to you is when you learn about my trainer's credentials. If you were to research the background of my trainer, you would find that he hadn't studied Plato, Socrates, Demming, or Drucker; nor does he have a Ph.D. or Master's Degree. In fact, it may surprise you to know that at the time I took the course, he hadn't even attended school.

You see, TCS Training stands for _**Tyler Curry Stevenson Training;**_ actually named after the instructor of the course. The instructor happened to be my **four-year-old son** _(at the time I wrote this)_, who has definitely put me through a rather rigorous training program since his birth.

In sitting down and looking back as to what I had learned from this DYNAMO, something else became obvious to me. I started to examine what Tyler had learned over the first few years of his life. He had learned how to speak a language, crawl, walk, ride a trike, sing, draw, count, feed himself, swim, the ABC's, go to the potty _(yeah)_, work the TV & VCR remote controls, turn my computer on and off _(not good)_, answer the phone, swing, climb, run, say please and thank you, give love/hugs and kisses, believe, imagine, play, and laugh.

What's really scary about all of this is that it's just a partial list of what he had learned. **I then started to compare what Tyler had learned in his first few years of life to what I had learned during that short time span; mine was pale by comparison.** My son is no longer four years old, but the training has still not stopped, and I hope it never does.

LINE RAISER:
If you want your _Line to Keep Rising_ you must keep learning.

CHAPTER 51
Why are Some People
More Successful Than Others

There are several reasons why some people are more successful than others. Successful people have PERSISTENCE, DESIRE, and ALWAYS GET UP WHEN KNOCKED DOWN (to name just a few of their character traits). Successful people understand that success comes to those who hang on longer than others. They have decided where it is they want to go and then go over, around, or through whatever obstacles stand in their way. This is the point I want to focus on ... **how they GET THERE.**

Every person has gifts and talents but it is up to them to hone these things in order to seize the opportunities they can bring. This honing ... practicing ... enhancing ... perfecting process is what separates those who succeed from those who don't. Your personal level of success is directly related to the amount of study and practice you put in.

I've already mentioned but it is worth repeating:

> Based on a 40-hour workweek, you would have approximately 1,960 work hours per year. According to a study by the American Society for Training and Development (ASTD) the average number of hours spent in a classroom by an American worker is 26.3 hours per year. That would mean the average American worker spends less than 1.5% of their workday perfecting their profession. Therefore, on average, American workers spend only 6.5 minutes per day developing their talent.

A gold medal gymnast training for a single Olympic event will have practiced their routine over 5,000 times and done over 100,000 repetitions of various skills. Janet Evans, a three-time Olympian and winner of four Olympic Gold Medals, swam over 45,000 miles in practice over her 12 year career. That means, every year for 12 years, she swam from Key West, Florida, to Seattle, Washington, and would still have another 400 miles to swim. Michael Phelps, who has won the most Olympic Gold Medals, (18 Gold and 22 Olympic medals in all) trained 6 hours per day, 6 days per week.

These facts should make it obvious that to be successful at anything requires a lot of practice. Whatever your profession is, athletic or non-athletic... if you don't practice you will not improve. **One well-developed talent/skill is worth far more than a hundred unrefined ones.** The choice is yours. You can stand out and be noticed as a true talent, or blend in with the multitude of average folks who just put in the bare minimum to get by. What are you doing every day to perfect your skills?

The defining moment in your journey towards the success you desire will be when you decide to put in the time to excel at your profession. You will be amazed what you can do when study and practice are part of your daily routine, which, by the way ... should never stop.

THERE IS NO SUCCESS WITHOUT PRACTICE

Michelangelo made incredible statues by chipping away at giant blocks of marble. He envisioned the finished piece before ever raising his mallet and kept chipping away until his *masterpiece* was completed. Every day you need to **chip away** at becoming better. If you intend to be successful, creating your own masterpiece, you don't do it overnight.

For over 24 years, I have been a professional speaker and have addressed the top companies in the world on numerous issues that would help their people perform at a higher level. In preparing for over 2,500 programs, not once have I had anyone tell me their people were lacking in the hard skills, technical knowledge, or the book sense they needed to succeed in their industry. Instead, I have always been asked to address subjects that have to deal with what is referred to as *soft skills*.

Unlike *hard skills*, which are about someone's skill and ability to perform a task, *soft skills* are more broadly applicable to successfully running an enterprise. *Soft skills* are the behavioral competencies people possess. Also known as *people skills or interpersonal skills*, they include talents such as strategic thinking, communication skills, team building, leadership and management skills, negotiation skills, conflict resolution, personal effectiveness, productive and inventive problem solving, along with selling skills, to name just a few. **Top executives understand that a person's** *soft skills* **are an important part of their individual contribution to the success of the organization.**

The mistake I see people and companies making is that they get consumed with dealing with everything else and not taking a few minutes each day to develop **soft skills.** You don't create these *soft skills* overnight. Keep in mind Michelangelo's method of creation; small chips carved away to uncover the beauty that was always there in his mind. Every day on a personal or corporate basis, make sure some sort of "Chipping Away" is taking place.

LINE RAISER:
Don't let a day go by that you or your employees have not gained "A Small Chip" of knowledge, skill, or talent.

Doing the little things can add up to great BIG results. Professor, author, and leadership expert, Dr. David Schwartz once said, *"The person determined to achieve maximum success learns the principle that progress is made one step at a time. Every big accomplishment is a series of little accomplishments."* One of the wealthiest men in the world, Warren Buffet, was once quoted as saying, *"I don't look to jump over 7-foot bars: I look around for 1-foot bars that I can step over."* But my favorite quote on this subject was made by Pastor Robert H. Schuller who said, *"Inch by inch, it's a cinch."*

Doing the Little Things - Makes Big Things Happen

There is NO immunity to having problems; successful people have problems, issues, complications, difficulties, set-backs, and make mistakes. They aren't immune to any of these things and having a great attitude doesn't protect them from having bad things happen to them, either; that "myth" is a total misnomer. Having a great attitude … helps you get over … the bad things that can happen to you. **Success is all about being able to deal with whatever is thrown at you.**

Here are a few more things successful people understand:

➢ The wiser a person gets the more they listen.

➢ Want to become great … copy what the great ones do.

➢ Those who complain a lot – succeed very little.

➢ Most people fail due to lack of effort - not lack of knowledge.

➢ If you want to get better - get out of your comfort zone.

➢ Do more than you are paid to do … every time.

➢ Do what you said you would do. Deliver every time.

➢ Your actions PROVE the type person you are.

➢ Most people are able to do a lot more ... they just aren't willing to.

➢ Failure, Mediocrity, and Success are in DIRECT relation to your effort.

➢ Never listen to those who have not done "IT" tell you how to do "IT."

➢ The sooner you admit you messed up - the sooner you can get on with fixing it.

➢ Discipline is a MUST. There is NO SUBSTITUTE for it. NONE!
   Those without discipline NEVER EXCEL.

➢ Take note of what others do that annoy you. Maybe you're doing things that annoy them. If you think not ... think again.

➢ Results are everything. You will be graded by what you do, not what you said you would do.

➢ For you whiners - 80% who hear you whine don't care.
                    19% are glad you are joining them.
                    1% will listen ... but wish they didn't have to.
                     So, try hard not to whine!

But, just because there is NO immunity to having problems, doesn't mean you can't avoid some of those problems. Some problems can be avoided with just a little insight. According to the American Booksellers Association … eighty percent of Americans did not buy or read a book this past year, and seventy percent of American adults have not bought a book in the past 5 years. By getting this far in my book, you already understand that you can gain SO MUCH experience, insight, and knowledge by reading about the experiences of others.

LINE RAISER:
You need to understand that you can
shorten your learning curve by
reading for **KNOWLEDGE** every day.
Make it part of your daily routine
and share the habit with others.

I am always looking for great quotes, saying, or statements to help reinforce my message, and I think it is important to give credit to those who shared their brilliance. Unfortunately, I often come across wise words of wisdom that have been credited to "ANONYMOUS." It sure would be nice to know who said such wise or clever words.

But, in all honesty, is a statement more profound, wise, brilliant, insightful, astute, sensible, intelligent, shrewd, smart, or clever, because a famous person said it? I don't think so. I think that each quote should stand alone, judged on its own merit, and not be given more or less value because of who said it.

Below are a few ***Anonymous Quotes*** I've collected over the years I thought you might find helpful:

> ➢ To be a winner, all you need to give is all you have.
> ➢ I have often regretted my speech, never my silence.
> ➢ For every action, there is an equal and opposite criticism.
> ➢ The best way to finish an unpleasant task is to get started.
> ➢ Minds are like parachutes - they only function when open.

➤ He is truly wise who gains wisdom from another's mishap.
➤ Stupid people always think they are right.
  Wise people listen to advice.
➤ Why do people say "no offense" right before they're about to offend you?
➤ Worry doesn't help tomorrow's troubles,
  but it does ruin today's happiness.
➤ Business is like a wheelbarrow.
  Nothing ever happens until you start pushing.
➤ If everything seems to be going well,
  you have obviously overlooked something.
➤ Everybody has the right to be stupid ...
  some people are just abusing the privilege.
➤ Set aside half an hour every day to do all your worrying;
  then take a nap during this period.
➤ When tempted to fight fire with fire,
  remember that the Fire Department usually uses water.
➤ Good judgment comes from experience, and experience –
  well, that comes from poor judgment.

LINE RAISER:

Go to school on other people's experiences.
Learn from their wise words or from their mistakes
and shorten your learning curve.
If I have learned one thing in business,
it is "WHY" experience the pain to learn something
when you don't have to; the more knowledge
you can gain from others, the better for you.

Life is too short to
learn and experience it ALL yourself.
Success comes to those
who seek knowledge from others and apply it.

CHAPTER 52
What Matters Most

I write a lot about leadership, management, efficiency, corporate culture, communication, personal growth, change, habits, choices, discipline, and how you can refine or develop these things so you can be more successful. Sometimes I think we forget "WHY" we do what we do and more importantly, who we are doing it for. I have been doing a lot of research on what people think really matters in life and over and over again, people kept saying ... **"The little things matter most."**

Spending time with my family and friends, long walks, watching the sunset or the sunrise, ice cream, the smell of fresh baked cookies, milkshakes, buying a pumpkin on Halloween to carve, laughter, smiles, good food, freedom, good health, riding my Harley, watching a great game on TV with my friends, a couple of cold beers and conversation, and celebrating the holidays with family, were just some of the many things people mentioned. I would like to note that no one mentioned being able to spend a few more hours in the office.

Charles Francis Adams was the grandson of the second President of the United States, John Adams. He was also a successful attorney, Congressman, and a former Ambassador to Great Britain. He was a very busy man who was consumed with success and had little time for his family. He did, however, keep a diary that he liked to write in as often as possible. One day he wrote this – *"Went fishing with my son today - a day wasted."* His son Brooks, also kept a diary, and the historians found on that same day, he too wrote in his diary. *"Went fishing with my father today - the most wonderful day of my life."* Don't let success in business take precedent over your family. Years ago I wrote, *"Success at the expense of your family is not true success."* I believe that more than ever today.

I think in business and in our personal lives we lose sight of the important people around us. We take those, who matter most, for granted. The more we take their love and support for granted ... not reciprocating in any manner ... the more we are pushing them away. Today, write down a list of those people around you who are important to you and start doing some "Simple – Special" things for them. Don't expect anything back for what you do for them … just open up and give. **Remember, giving to get something is not truly giving.**

Little gestures of support and kindness, listening while not judging, helping hands, remembering birthdays and anniversaries for family, friends and associates, hand written notes of support or thanks, simple gifts, baking cookies for the office, buying a birthday cake for an associate at the office, going fishing or to the fair with your kids … can be simple for you and mean SO MUCH to them.

My son Tyler just walked into my office and asked me if I could knock off work early today. I looked up and said, *"Sure."* His face filled with a big smile and he said, *"Great."* There was a time when I would have said, *"Not today, Buddy. Daddy is just too busy."* But now, thank goodness, I have come to realize there will come a day (way to soon) when he won't be around to ask that question; he will be busy with his life and family. I am trying harder and harder to make the things in life that really matter … a PRIORITY … you should, too.

LINE RAISER:
**Start doing the simple things with those special to you.
Let them see they matter most, by what you do.**

A lot of people get confused with what should come first – Success or Happiness?

This isn't going to be a *"what comes first"* – the Chicken or the Egg debate. There is actually some excellent data that answers our title question. Dr. Sonja Lybomirsky, of the University of California, along with several colleagues, analyzed the results of 211 different studies addressing this issue.

They wanted to know:

Are happy people more successful?
and
Does happiness precede success?

The results of their extensive research showed ... happiness leads to greater success ... happy people have more positive moods ... positive moods prompt people to work actively and reach new goals. Happy people are more productive, more innovative, communicate better, more respected, more appreciated, more optimistic, more energetic, more likable, more confident, and more sociable. WOW, that is quite an impressive list. All of these attributes help to make us more successful. Happy people also have less stress, but with a million workers per day missing work due to stress, it is evident there are a lot of unhappy people out there.

In a business world where companies are downsizing their staffs ... this simply means they are also upsizing the workloads for those employees who stay. The greater the demand placed on employees the greater the potential for *"even more"* stress, and more stress leads to less happiness. Then, add to the equation supporting your family, unexpected expenses, rising household costs, rising health insurance costs, a lousy economy *(etc.)* and the priority of trying to be happy takes a distant second place to merely surviving. The attitude of ... ***I don't have time to worry about being happy – I'm too busy working ... becomes our mindset.***

I remember years ago when the billionaire Howard Hughes died, a reporter asked, ***"How much money did Mr. Hughes leave behind?"*** The person responded, ***"All of it."*** What a great answer. If I can share anything with you today, it would be on the importance of YOUR HAPPINESS. Your happiness will energize you in everything you do, so work on that. Lighten up. Laugh more. Start counting your blessings. Be grateful. Be optimistic. Your stress level will go down, your productivity will go up and everyone around you will be better off because of your happiness. Remember, happy people have problems too, they just handle them differently.

One last bit of information for you; **DON'T BE A PROFESSIONAL DEPRESSION** ... a person who just can't seem to find the positive in anything. Happiness starts with the words you speak ... so before opening your mouth to let someone know the traffic was terrible, the clerk at the store was a jerk, the bank bounced your check, you couldn't find a parking space close to the store, you missed your plane, etc., etc., etc. ... understand you are now reliving the bad things that just happened to you ... so they live on ... you just multiplied their effects. Don't do that. It brings you down again and ALSO brings down the person you are sharing them with ... and that is not fair.

LINE RAISER:

At the end of the day, our happiness and the happiness of our family is all that matters.

Everything else is commentary.

CHAPTER 53
Our Choices Show Who We Are

People have asked me time-and-time-again, *"What is the most important habit you need to have to be successful?"* My answer to that specific question is, DISCIPLINE. But, I must give a caveat to my response. You see, I believe there can be no REAL SUCCESS without INTEGRITY. I used the words *"REAL SUCCESS,"* because I know there are a lot of people out there, whom to many people, would seem extremely successful.

I guess if you measure success by wealth, money or possessions, then they would be successful. But, I don't see success that way. To me, this chapter is the most important chapter of my book; that is why I saved it until last. The choices you make in life will determine your REAL success.

LINE RAISERS:

Choose to   not live a life of mediocrity
Choose to   not argue about trivial things
Choose to   not worry, fret, or cry about small injustices
Choose to   not let others control your destiny
Choose to   never give up
Choose to   never quit learning
Choose to   be punctual, orderly, and diligent
Choose to   believe in yourself
Choose to   live a life of action not words
Choose to   practice, drill, and rehearse
Choose to   be a positive person
Choose to   guard your integrity

And by making these choices, you have now chosen to be successful.

I think the following poem I wrote will help to give you a better understanding as to the importance I place on integrity and how it should guide the choices we make.

Integrity is a Choice

A choice is not a simple thing because consequences will matter,
when making a decision clear your mind of all needless chatter.
It's your future you're affecting by the decisions you make,
it's your future you're creating – so you don't want to make a mistake.

We all must know that in the end our choices decide who we are,
some choices are right, some choices are wrong, and some will leave a scar.
It is you who will decide how you live your life,
in many cases your choices will decide how much happiness or strife.

There will be things that happen that you did not choose,
but how you choose to handle them will determine if you win or lose.
So never look for the half-truth or the easy way out,
because the decisions you make will tell us what you're all about.

If you decide to look the other way and make no choice at all,
having no courage to choose will be the cause of your downfall.
I choose to live my life as if I were on stage,
that every choice I make will reveal my character gauge.

For once you make the decision, you choose what to do,
your integrity is now made public, there is no hiding it from view.
Understand the life you live is really not by chance,
your success or failure comes from how you take a stance.

So make your choices following one powerful guiding light,
search for truth, honesty and fairness, and then decide what's right.
By taking this course of action, you will never be wrong,
for true success comes to only those willing to be strong.

Integrity/character, or should I say – *lack thereof* – is being revealed to us daily. From the house painter who said they would prime before they painted (and they didn't), to the mechanic who replaces your carburetor when only the fuel line was clogged. Their character has just been revealed; they chose to cheat you.

Here is an analogy I found a few years ago that I think gives us a great example about having integrity and good character.

Character is Displayed at the Bottom of the Basket

It's just a simple purchase ... a basket of peaches at the local farmers market. The peaches on the top, and even in the middle are all beautiful ... but the farmer's character is revealed with the fruit they placed on the bottom of the basket. The fruit on the bottom should be just as good as the fruit on top, but a farmer of weak character will put the bruised (damaged) fruit on the bottom. A butcher can put the best looking side of the steak face up, so you see it through the clear plastic, but when you get home, you find the underneath side full of gristle and fat; again, a weak character is revealed.

Clothes style change, fads change, hair styles change, popular music choices change, technology changes, car models change, expectations, salaries and opinions all change ... **but good character should never change. Actions indicate CHARACTER ... not words.**

Good character isn't hard to identify ... it is simply doing the right thing even when it may be the hardest thing to do. Good, sound, strong, morale character is a choice ... you can choose to have it or not. That painter, mechanic, farmer, and butcher all made a choice, and their choice instantly revealed their character. It would also give me a good reason to NEVER want to do business with them again. *Fool me once, shame on you – Fool me twice, shame on me.*

Here are a few of my thoughts on the importance I place on character.

THE MARK YOU LEAVE

Fame is fleeting, popularity, notoriety,
and wealth can leave you too.
Even your good health can slip away
and there's nothing you can do.

There are those who will sing your praises
for what you did today.
Then curse your actions tomorrow
and there's nothing you can say.

So heed my words carefully,
they are simple but oh so true.
You reveal your character daily
in everything you do.

Guard your thoughts, words and actions,
for they shout loudly who you are.
Your actions reveal your character
and will be seen both near and far.

And when you leave this earth,
there is but one thing that will endure.
Your character will be the mark you leave,
on this you can be sure.

I want to do business with people who are trustworthy, reliable, responsible, and considerate ... those actions will establish a fine reputation. Isn't it amazing what **just one bad peach** tells about a person.

Your Choices Define Your Character
So Choose Wisely

In order to advance your career and be truly successful in life, I think it is critical that you align yourself with people of integrity. *Built to Last, Competing for the Future, Competitive Advantage, Good to Great, In Search of Excellence, One Minute Manager, Seven Habits of Highly Effective People, Tipping Point,* and *The New Age of Innovation* are just a few of the books listed in the Top Business Books ever written. You might agree or disagree with the list; that is not important. What is important is what do they have in common? When I am reading a book or article about management, leadership, or peak performance, I am always looking for what they have in common with what other great scholars, leaders, or business icons have said; *I believe there is power in a point that is repeated over and over again by different sources.*

I also look for people who are revered, respected, admired, and often quoted by those great scholars, leaders, and business icons. One such person is the great management guru, Peter Drucker. This is a man who has been honored with over 25 honorary doctorates, written 39 books, and translated in over 30 languages. In one of his books, ***The Daily Drucker,*** he compiled a summary of his most important points from the over 10,000 pages of his insights on business.

His first point in this incredible book was based on INTEGRITY. He said, *"Align yourself with people of integrity."* Out of over 10,000 pages of insights, the first and most important point he wanted to make was based on integrity. In a world of uncertainty, incredible competition, ever-changing technology and government regulations, his first point was based on hiring the RIGHT people – those with INTEGRITY. He goes on to say …

"Surround yourself with people who will tell you the truth and allow them the platform to do so."

Mr. Drucker sums it up perfectly when he stated:

"Management is doing things right.
Leadership is doing the right things."

LINE RAISER:
It takes years to build a great reputation
and only moments to destroy it.
Always base your decisions on maintaining
the highest level of integrity.

The idiom *"Do as I say, not as I do,"* first appeared in John Selden's Table-Talk (c. 1654): simply meaning, **don't imitate my behavior, but obey my instructions.** Boy, does this seem to be the norm in the world today; politicians, bosses, teachers, coaches, associates, friends, and family members all telling us what to do, but not following their own suggestions, advice, directions, or instructions.

Just remember... someone is watching you and listening to what you say all the time. It seems everywhere we turn today people are challenging the truthfulness, accuracy, or validity of what people are saying. Thomas Jefferson once said, *"In matters of principle, stand like a rock ... Never suppose, that in any possible situation, or under any circumstances, it is best for you to do a dishonorable thing."* I believe you can seriously complicate matters and make things a great deal worse, when you try and manipulate your words to take the sting out of what really happened. Sometimes, the truth is going to hurt, so deal with it.

I am not a real fan of having to admit when I am wrong or I messed up, but I have found that you can get over the pain a lot faster by just telling it like it is. Take your lumps and bumps if you messed up. You deserve them. You messed up. It's that simple. Years ago I had been personally been wronged by an individual. It took a few days for the real truth to come out and destroy what little integrity the person had, but it was a tough few days. After I calmed down, I sat down and wrote this poem, not just to reflect on what had happened, but to share how I feel about the importance of truthfulness.

THE ONLY WAY

The truth is but a simple thing, for it knows no right or wrong.

There are those who would alter it, to make the truth be gone.

They will speak, imply, suggest what you know are not the facts.

But the truth will remain the same, rest assured it will be back.

It may be for the moment, the truth is not revealed.

There you stand betrayed by one, accused of what's not real.

But for those of us who have been wronged, take solace in what I say.

There will come a time where all will know, in some uncertain way.

The truth will rise above it all, and prove their words were wrong.

Causing those who spoke the words, reputations now be gone.

The truth is but a simple thing, it may be hard to say,

The truth is but a simple thing, and for me the only way.

There is no reason to complicate the truth. My dad once told me, ***"Son, you don't have to have a perfect memory, if you just tell it like it is."*** What he was simply saying was …if someone asks you what happened, tell them. If someone else asks you what happened, you don't have to recall what you said previously. The story (the truth) will always be the same. You should assume everything you do will someday end up in some sort of social media with a detailed accounting of your actions … so act accordingly.

Honesty, Integrity, Honor
can never be taken away, only given up.
So guard them dearly, for once given up,
they can never be returned.

So many people and companies speak of greatness but never achieve it. So many leaders push, demand, strive, wish, and hope for greatness but never accomplish it. Greatness isn't accomplished by command, it's accomplished by desire and a willingness to do what is necessary to achieve it. You will know you are a great leader, manager, teacher, or coach when you start helping those around you become better. Encouraging, assisting, and inspiring people are far more effective than DEMANDING excellence. I know one thing to be true about greatness:

Greatness is within you,
in this I have **NO DOUBT**,
Greatness is within you,
but only "YOU" can pull it out.

Remember, in your journey towards success, only "YOU" can **_Raise Your Line_**. On the next and final page of my book, I would like to leave you with my **Success Challenge**.

Challenges are what make life interesting.
Overcoming them is what makes it meaningful.

Success Challenge

While others complain	look for alternatives and solutions
While others make excuses	accept responsibility, correct and move on
While others show up late	always be early and prepared
While others find fault	look for advantages and strengths
While others blame someone else	strive to exonerate and help
While others gossip	stay silent
While others lie	always be truthful
While others fail to study	read, research and review
While others have no purpose	establish a plan and do it
While others doubt their ability	have confidence you will succeed
While others procrastinate	move forward and persist
While others are inflexible	be tolerant, reasonable and cooperative
While others shirk responsibility	be accountable for your actions and duties
While others ridicule	compliment, respect and praise
While others do the bare minimum	always do more than expected
While others never volunteer	try to always lend a helping hand
While others waste time	be focused, efficient and organized
While others are negative	be positive
While others are fearful	have courage
While others compromise their integrity	guard it at all cost
While others give up	try again

Accept this challenge and you will
RAISE YOUR LINE.

Good luck!

About the Author

Robert Stevenson is an expert at building a high performance culture, improving efficiency, and accelerating growth. He is one of the most widely sought after speakers in the world today, as well as a best-selling author. He has owned five companies, sold internationally in over 20 countries, along with holding positions from Salesman to Chief Executive Officer.

Robert has spoken to over 2,500 companies throughout the world and his research in the area of corporate and entrepreneurial success is extensive. Over 2 million people have benefitted from his powerful, practical, compelling and thought-provoking programs. He has interviewed over 10,000 employees, managers, and senior executives in over 250 industries. He calls upon his knowledge of what he has learned from some of the most innovative, resourceful, and powerful companies in the world, along with what he learned running his own companies and shares this wisdom with his audiences. He is a true master at blending facts, inspiration, conviction, and humor into all his programs.

Robert's lectures are designed to prepare companies for the 21st century. With a powerful blend of experience, research, case studies, and competitor perspectives, Robert's original insights help organizations, business leaders, and associates understand how to unleash their future potential. With over 30 years of extensive corporate and entrepreneurial experience, he teaches companies and people how to deal with risk, competition, and the ever-changing business environment.

Mr. Stevenson's client list reads like a Who's Who in business. Companies like FedEx, Prudential, Lockheed Martin, Carrier, Anheuser-Busch, Chevron, American Express, and Berkshire Hathaway continue to rely on him for a fresh, unique perspective on businesses' most crucial issues. If you would like to receive information about Mr. Stevenson's books, training DVDs, or how to hire him to work with your organization, you can reach him at:

info@robertstevenson.org

(727) 789–2727

www.RobertStevenson.org